Cool Parents, Drug-Free Kids

A Family Survival Guide

Robert Holman Coombs
University of California at Los Angeles

Allyn and Bacon

Boston ■ London ■ Toronto ■ Sydney ■ Tokyo ■ Singapore

For
Karen, David, and Kristina

Executive Editor: Carolyn Merrill
Editorial Assistant: Lara Zeises
Production Editor: Michelle Limoges
Production Manager: Susan Brown
Electronic Composition: Peggy Cabot, Cabot Computer Services
Composition and Prepress Buyer: Linda Cox
Manufacturing Buyer: JoAnne Sweeney
Cover Administrator: Kristina Mose-Libon

Between the time website information is gathered and then published, it is not
unusual for some sites to have closed. Also, the transcription of URLs can result in
unintended typographical errors. The publisher would appreciate notification
where these occur so that they may be corrected in subsequent editions.

Library of Congress Cataloging-in-Publication Data

Coombs, Robert H.
    Cool parents, drug-free kids : a family survival guide / Robert Holman
Coombs.
      p. cm.
    Includes bibliographical references and index.
    ISBN 0-205-32482-7 (alk. paper)
      1. Children—Drug use—United States. 2. Drug abuse—United States—
Prevention. 3. Parenting—United States. I. Title.

HV5824.C45 C667 2001
649'.4—dc21
                                                            2001018821

Printed in the United States of America

10 9 8 7 6 5 4 3 2 1   06 05 04 03 02 01

CONTENTS

PREFACE

If you suspect that your son or daughter is using drugs, go directly to Part Seven of this book and begin reading Chapters 17–21.* Get help quickly! If your child is in junior or senior high school and you feel estranged from him or her, start with Part Five (Chapters 9–13). These action chapters will help you strengthen your relationships and increase your influence. Then go back to the earlier chapters to gain an understanding about what psychoactive drugs are, why kids use them, how young people can escalate into deeper involvement with drugs, and which major industries provide drugs and encourage their use.

It's a challenge to raise healthy, content, and chemically free youngsters in a turbulent world where drugs are readily available and widely glamorized. Parenting today is much more complicated than it once was. How can you and your family survive in these challenging times?

I wrote this book to show parents how to help their kids get high on healthy living and to avoid chemically induced highs that undermine health and well-being. Although directed toward teens and their parents, most of the information and recommendations herein are equally applicable to young adults. *Cool Parents, Drug-Free Kids* summarizes more than twenty-five years of my research and reflections about the processes of drug involvement. I have extensively reviewed other researchers' findings and conducted my own long-term studies of teenagers, compared users and nonusers, and interviewed parents.** In addition, I have spoken with dozens of addicted professionals—doctors, dentists, lawyers, nurses, pharmacists, and airline pilots—to learn about their family origins and the processes by which they got into and out of addictive lifestyles. I have participated as a nonaddicted observer in several drug-treatment programs, taught parent-training classes, and written books and many other publications about drug use and other related topics. Most important, I struggled as a father to raise my own children. Like anyone else, I wasn't a perfect parent, and I learned more from my mistakes than successes. Unfortunately, as one father noted, "Kids don't come with a manual."

---

*This book is primarily for parents. If your loved one on drugs is an adult—a parent, spouse, sibling, friend, or associate—read two of my recent books: *Drug-Impaired Professionals* (Harvard University Press, 1997) and *Addiction Recovery Tools: A Practical Handbook* (Sage, 2001). They will give you direction and help you understand the dynamics of addiction.

**Quotations from published sources are referenced. All unreferenced quotations cited in this book come from my personal files of tape-recorded interviews with teens, young adults, parents, addicts, and the clinicians who treat them.

If you are struggling as a parent, hoping to keep your kids safe and drug free, you are not alone. Drug abuse is a symptom of our challenging times. Unfortunately, whatever your family's problems are, they will be worse if your kids use chemical substances. Psychoactive drugs provide artificial highs—short-lived moments or hours of euphoria that are mere substitutes for the natural highs that come when youngsters feel nurtured, cared for, and successful.

I hope that in reading this book you feel encouraged, learn new ways to strengthen your family, and perhaps find a new sense of direction. If you do all the exercises at the end of each chapter, I predict that you and your family will grow significantly.

ACKNOWLEDGMENTS

I gratefully acknowledge:

Glen Stenhouse, an Auckland, New Zealand educator who initially urged me to write this book.

Carolyn Merrill, executive editor at Allyn & Bacon and Lara Zeises, her assistant, for their support and editorial direction. I also thank Michelle Limoges, production editor at Allyn & Bacon, and Laurie Johnson, copy editor, for polishing the manuscript and moving it along toward publication.

The many parents, students, and addicts who anonymously shared with me their personal experiences and insights.

Gareth Lacy, Claudia Agaze, and Grace Lee, my UCLA honors students, for gathering valuable library and Internet materials and inspiring me with their questions and fresh insights.

Tim Hoover, superb addiction counselor, for his penetrating perspectives on teenage addicts and ways to help them recover.

Chad Sorenson, of Sorenson's Ranch School, Koosharem, Utah, for sharing his wisdom and experiences operating an excellent adolescent residential treatment program.

Kim Barrus, Ph.D., psychotherapist, and Walter Felder for helpful insights and for reviewing the manuscript.

Donna M. and William Mapes, good friends, for sustained help and encouragement on several revisions of this manuscript, and for locating useful Internet materials.

Felipe Santana, my friend and clinical model, for teaching me so much about family health and impairment.

David C. Baugh, executive at CHOICE Humanitarian, for providing invaluable information about service opportunities in Third-World countries.

Kathryn Coombs, my daughter, a teacher, published author, and editor extraordinaire, for her creative ideas, her development of the chapter activities, and for thorough copyediting.

Loni, Karen, Holly, and Krista, my other daughters, and my sons, Bob and David, for their friendship and for sharing their lives with me.

Carla Cronkhite Vera, my invaluable UCLA assistant who, for more than a decade, helped develop this book by locating sources, checking references, obtaining permissions, typing numerous revisions, and handling a myriad other details—all with efficiency and good cheer.

Carol Jean Cook Coombs, my life partner, who also works with me at UCLA, for participating in every decision about this book; advising me; and providing help, support, and encouragement throughout.

x

PART ONE

What Are the Rewards and Costs of Using Psychoactive Drugs?

Daily accounts of drug problems in America fill our newspapers and other media. This week's clippings, as I write this, include these comments:

- "California public schools reported an increase in violent crime and drug and alcohol offenses last year, and a decrease in property crimes, according to a new state report. . . ."
- "We are obviously disappointed that drugs and alcohol are up and battery is up," said Delaine Eastin, State Superintendent of Public Instruction (Kim, 2000, p. A3).
- "It concerns me that we're running above the statewide average in alcohol and drug use," lamented the County Superintendent of Schools. Noting that drug use rises when state funding for antidrug and alcohol education declines, he explained, "What the legislators don't realize is that you never fix alcohol and drug use among minors because you constantly have new kids. It has to be a continued, sustained effort. . . . [W]e must continue to invest in these [antidrug education] programs so that we don't lose another generation of kids—any kids—to alcohol or drugs" (Raisin, 2000, p. 1).

Federal officials who regularly track teenage drug use crow when the national rates drop, as they occasionally do. These highly variable statistics go up and down from one survey to another. The latest national figures, for example, show that while use of some drugs among adolescents is currently down (cigarettes and marijuana), use of others (binge drinking and Ecstasy) has risen.

Although statistics tell us what has happened among large groups of people, they obscure the painful realities that confront individuals and their

1

families. When drug abuse happens in your family, it's not a one-percent statistical loss; it's a 100-percent personal loss.

Sidebar 1: Rachael's Story

In a recent three year period, more than 40 young people from and around Plano, Texas (near Dallas) died of heroin overdoses. "It's really frustrating," said a counselor at a drug rehab center. "We lose a lot of kids. Either they disappear or they die." One of them, 16-year-old Rachel H., a heroin addict, first smoked pot when she was 11. "When I was 12, I started doing acid and coke and speed," she acknowledged. "I remember on my 13th birthday, I was supposed to shoot up for the first time."

Her parents don't understand why their daughter turned to drugs. "It's not like she was a child of abuse who wasn't loved and adored," said her mother, a licensed therapist. "To this day, I'm not sure what she was missing that turned her to that." Desperate, her parents tried everything—counseling, boarding school, even a house alarm system to keep her drug-using friends away—but nothing seemed to work. Rachel avoided and escaped these unwanted intrusions and sometimes stayed away for home for as long as a month. "I'd stay up for seven or eight nights at a time, doing speed and cocaine, she said. "Drugs made me feel better," she added. "If I had a hard day, I'd say, 'I'm going to go get high.' That was my attitude, my mentality."

Rachael has been clean for almost a year after being shaken when her friend died of an overdose. "When Stephanie died, that was definitely my wake-up call," she said. But, as a drug counselor points out, *getting* clean is far easier than *staying* clean. "Getting clean is pretty easy, he said, "Staying clean is the meat and potatoes. . . . It's a lot easier to use drugs than to change.

David Kohn, 1999. "Kicking the Habit, Plano, Texas" CBS News Broadcasts, February 18, http://cbsnews.com/now/story/0,1597,140849-412,00.00.shtml.

The best place to start preventing drug problems with your kids is to understand what makes them use alcohol and other psychoactive drugs. Chapter 1 addresses the question: What motivates young drug users? Chapter 2 highlights the personal price users pay for these rewards.

REFERENCES

Kim, Ann L. 2000. "Schools Report Rise in Drug Crime, Violence." *Los Angeles Times,* March 1, pp. A3, A14.

Kohn, David. 1999. "Kicking the Habit, Plano, Texas." CBS News Broadcasts, Feb. 18.

Raisin, Amy. 2000. "Student Drug Use Rises." *Daily News* (Conejo Valley edition), March 1, pp. 1–2.

1 Rewards That Motivate Drug Users

Three kinds of rewards motivate young people to experiment with drugs: (1) *recreational* rewards, which involve fun and enjoyable activities with others; (2) *therapeutic* rewards, which elevate mood and provide relief from painful feelings of insecurity, doubt, and depression; and (3) *instrumental* (achievement) rewards, which temporarily enhance energy and improve performance. Each of these rewards can have great appeal, especially during adolescence.

Sidebar 1.1: Who Experiments With Mind–altering Drugs?

There are two kinds of children who use drugs . . . GIRLS and BOYS (Boswell, n.d.).

Being accepted and liked by others is critically important during one's teen years, a period of self-consciousness when most people keenly feel anticipation of rejection. Nearly half of all Americans (48 percent) feel imprisoned by shyness (Carducci, 2000). Shy people unrealistically compare themselves unfavorably to the most socially outstanding person, the life of the party. To make matters worse, they attribute their own social performance to unchanging, internal shortcomings (for example, "I just can't talk to people"). This only heightens their self-consciousness, making it even harder for them to interact smoothly with others (Carducci, 2000).

Most shy people—91 percent in one study—try to overcome their shyness by going to parties, bars, dances, a mall, and other places where they will be around others. But they typically expect others to take the initiative, to approach them and draw them out of their shyness. To compound this problem, shy people tend to subject themselves to perfectionistic standards. Believing that everyone is watching and judging them, they think their comments must be perfect—witty, wise, and wonderful. Because this rarely, if ever, happens (for anybody), they castigate themselves with negative self-talk: "I can't believe I said that. Now they all think I'm a real loser."

Chemical Magic

Many adolescents and others try to solve these kinds of problems with a quick fix: alcohol and other psychoactive drugs, called "liquid extroversion" (Carducci, 2000). These "social lubricants" suppress shyness; quiet inner, critical voices; and release social inhibitions.

"A significant proportion of problem drinkers in the general population are shy," reports psychological researcher Bernardo Carducci (2000, p. 43). "They believe that people will like them only if they are outgoing, not the way they really are." So they turn to alcohol and other psychoactive drugs, which seem to create personality transformations and miraculously ease uncomfortable feelings—at least initially. Feelings of inferiority and other painful emotions magically disappear, and a new personality, free from fear and anxiety, seems to blossom.

Why is adolescence the time most people begin using drugs? Of all life stages, the teenage years are when we long to be accepted, and when we struggle most with self-esteem issues. Like a magic wand promising confidence and fun, alcohol and other drugs can appeal strongly to young people. It's no wonder that reliance on mood-altering substances can become a way of life, as this adult recalled:

> Whenever I had a date and wanted to be on my best, on top of my form, I could self-medicate. Whenever I felt a little nervous, I had an excuse to use. If a test was coming up and I was a little bit uptight about the exam, I would use stimulants. Whenever I didn't feel comfortable or in control of the situation—pretty much all of my life—I would use that as an excuse to use drugs. That was my pattern pretty much all the way through school (Coombs & Ziedonis, 1995, p. 60).

Acutely desiring peer approval, kids can easily come to regard alcohol and other drugs as their "best friend." "It allowed me to feel at ease in social situations where I normally would be uncomfortable," one explained. "It helped me belong and have peer approval and not be different," another remarked. "After downing my first glass of beer, I felt I fit in."

Sidebar 1.2: Feeling Okay About Self

"I didn't have a clue in the world how to deal with people. I always felt like an outsider. My family had moved a couple of crucial times in my life and I didn't have any long-term friends. But with alcohol, I felt fine. It was my way to feel okay for the first time in my young life."

So great is the desire for social success that even kids who initially have bad experiences with alcohol may keep drinking. "My first drink was brandy and that made me violently ill," said one student. "I ended up throwing up and lying in my friend's bed with the lightbulb spinning. It was really a terrible experience." Undaunted, however, he continued trying until he had "mastered" drinking. "Although I have a vivid recollection of getting sick," he explained, "the most vivid recollection was feeling like I was one of the boys. I'd always had some difficulty in peer interaction and when I drank the alcohol, it filled that void. It helped me feel at ease" (Coombs, 1997, p. 41).

Some teens use drugs—tobacco for example—to decrease their appetite and thus lose weight. This makes them look more like the skinny models featured in today's media. Others use drugs to enhance their school or athletic performance. Stimulants make it possible to study longer, work longer and harder, concentrate better, and accomplish more—at least for a while. Unprepared for tomorrow's examination, a student may pull an all-nighter under the influence of a stimulant.

Many professional athletes use stimulants to gain a competitive edge. Although sports organizations have banned stimulants, anabolic agents,* diuretics,** street drugs, and analogues,*** many young people still seek those drugs to improve their own athletic performance. Mark McGwire, who set a new home-run record after using a now illegal over-the-counter drug, influenced an entire generation of admiring young Americans. Preoccupied with body appearance, teens use steroids to contour their muscles or lower their percentage of body fat. Gazing at fitness magazines, kids see body builders who, though they no longer take steroids, admit to having used them in the past. Kids ask, "If they did it, why not me?"

Party Scenes

Social settings provide arenas where teens and young adults simultaneously experience all three rewards. When together with their peers, they often find that alcohol and other psychoactive drugs help them have fun with others (recreational rewards), fit in (achievement rewards) and forget their shyness, self-doubts, and inhibitions (therapeutic rewards).

---

*Synthetic derivatives of testosterone which promote skeletal muscle growth.

**So-called "water pills" that help the body rid excess water and salt by excreting it through urine.

***Sometimes called "designer drugs," they are made slightly different from parent compounds so they are temporarily immune from DEA control.

"Rave parties," the current rage among teenagers and young adults, provide these rewards. Ecstasy and other party drugs allow party-goers to reduce their anxieties, have fun, fit in with a particular group of peers, and dance all night.

Ecstasy comes in two forms: press pills and a powder that is either snorted through the nose or ingested. Selling for anywhere between $15 and $40 per "hit" (one-tenth of a gram), the drug has an effect, like that of cocaine or other stimulants, that may last as long as six hours.

Rave parties usually begin after midnight and can attract up to fifteen thousand people. On weekends in such places as warehouses, clubs, factories, or vacant churches—party organizers usually conceal the location until that day to heighten the excitement and fend off authorities—kids dance through the night to loud music. Because Ecstasy dehydrates the body, empty water bottles litter the floors and sparkle in the hands of dancers. One participant describes the experience:

> You pay $25 bucks for a tiny pill . . . wash it down with a liter of water, then sit back and wait for the magic to happen. Within an hour a feeling of euphoria starts spreading through your limbs and scalp and fingertips. You feel a previously unknown dose of esteem that cues you to talk to strangers about the brand-new wonderful thoughts colliding in your head. Someone offers to brush your hair; you let him, and it's about the most sensual thing you've ever felt. You can dance all night, expressing your bliss by flailing your arms and riding to the driving beat of a non-stop techno tune. You become best friends with people whose names you don't bother to learn. You become part of a train of people who are massaging each other's shoulders, partly because it feels good to you and partly because you want to do something gratifying for someone else. You want to be nice (www.connectsavannah.com).

Sidebar 1.3: A Raver's Opinion

"Cocaine, the drug of choice of the '80s 'Me' generation, makes users feel confident and invincible. The high from [E]cstasy is almost the opposite; it is the 'We' drug, urging individuals to step outside themselves and enjoy a communal experience" (www.theage.com.au/).

This is all harmless fun, most ravers think, because Ecstasy, also called a "love drug," heightens feelings of warmth and affection on the dance floor. This effect enhances users' social lives and makes them feel as if they are everyone's friend. "I felt confident in the knowledge that if I shunned hypodermic needles and drug dealers dressed in black and lurking in poorly lit alleyways, my future was secure," reasoned a young participant (www.theage.com.au/).

Dancing through the night, kids are blissfully unaware that they are contributing to a multimillion-dollar illicit business. In Toronto, for example, police busted up a $1.5 million-a-week Ecstasy organization (www. mapping.org/drugnews/v99/n1262/A09.html).

When vacationing in Whistler, British Columbia, I read this report about a local rave party. "By the time the RCMP [Royal Canadian Mounted Police] showed up, tipped off by an anonymous source, there were already more than 1,000 people in attendance at the all-night party, some who paid $40 to get in. . . . [T]here was minimal security and only two first-aid attendants who were attempting to stabilize an unconscious girl whose pulse rate was low when RCMP arrived." Someone had called an ambulance, but more than 250 cars parked along the road blocked access. "This is an organization," the report says, "that comes to a community, rapes it, and leaves nothing behind but a lot of garbage" (Mitchell, 2000, p. 13).

Can a substance also called the "Hug Drug" be bad? ravers question. If a drug helps me overcome my shyness and promotes positive, friendly feelings, how can it possibly be harmful? Seduced by such logic and the supposed social value of these parties, some parents offer little resistance. A twenty-year-old paramedic who worked his first (and last) rave was astounded when parents dropped off their youngsters at these events. "They come down . . . in their Lexus' or their Blazers to pick up their kids. . . . What are they thinking?" A steady stream of kids, mostly semiconscious and brought by their friends or security, came to his ambulance, which was parked outside the main entrance.

Although his job required writing up every problem incident, this paramedic found it difficult to obtain important information, because raving is an underground activity. "[The kids] were very vague and evasive," he complained. "They wouldn't sign anything or tell us their names." So, unfortunately, he could not take them to the hospital. After a bit of oxygen and a rest, most went back to the party. Cast into the role of enabling "a night of excess" made the young man profoundly uncomfortable, and he resolved never to do it again (www.canoe.ca/TorontoSun.com).

While consulting at a drug rehabilitation center, I met a handsome young medical student who had become addicted to Ecstasy at rave parties. His schooling and career on hold, he will spend several months in treatment trying to straighten out his life. He, like the other addicts there—mostly physicians and other professionals—mistakenly thought that psychoactive drugs made life better. Only later did he discover the terrible price he and his loved ones would pay when the "magic wand" turned out to be Pandora's box instead.

ACTIVITIES FOR PARENTS AND KIDS

1.1   Write down everything you think you've taught your kids about drugs and alcohol. At the same time, have your kids write down what they think you've taught them. Compare and contrast your answers.

1.2   Ask your kids why they think kids use drugs. Later, discuss with them what this chapter has to say.

1.3   Ask each family member to bring a current drug-related news item (a newspaper clipping or an account of an event at school) to the dinner table. Show the items and discuss the events.

1.4   Describe times when family members might feel shy or socially awkward; for example,

- being at a party,
- asking a question in class,
- being with someone you want to impress,
- making a presentation at school or work,
- feeling pressured by a friend to do something you would rather not or are not sure you want to do, or
- other times.

1.5   Share your own experiences about feeling self-conscious as a child, including some embarrassing moment(s) and the ways in which you dealt with them. Talk about times you felt socially awkward or self-conscious, and describe what you did about it. Praise each other's coping skills!

1.6   Tell kids the secret of adult life: that peer pressure and popularity contests will always go on, but that you learn to handle them better. Tell about times you have felt self-conscious or embarrassed as an adult, and explain how you dealt with it.

REFERENCES

Boswell, Vesta. PRYDE in New Zealand (pamphlet), National Resource Centre, Oxford Street, P.O. Box 32, Lyttelton, N.Z. (E-mail: pryde@ihng.co.nz).

Carducci, Bernardo. 2000. "The New Solution." *Psychology Today*, January/February, pp. 39–45, 78.

Coombs, Robert H. 1997. *Drug-Impaired Professionals*. Cambridge, MA: Harvard University Press.

Coombs, Robert H. & Ziedonis, Douglas. 1995. *Handbook on Drug-Abuse Prevention: A Comprehensive Strategy to Prevent the Abuse of Alcohol and Other Drugs*. Boston: Allyn & Bacon.

Mitchell, Andrew. 2000. "RCMP Consider Charges Against Rave Organizers." *Pique Magazine*, July 14, p. 13.

INTERNET SOURCES

www.canoe.ca/TorontoSun.com
www.connectsavannah.com
www.mapping.org/drugnews/v99/n1262/A09.html
www.theage.com.au/

CHAPTER

2 The Price of Drug Abuse

Most teens who experiment with alcohol and other psychoactive drugs experience the benefits described in the last chapter. It is not surprising then that some continue using and even escalate their drug use, perhaps thinking, "It can only get better." Inevitably, however, the tide turns, particularly for frequent users. It's like borrowing on a credit card to wear elegant clothes, drive a hot car, eat out every night: Eventually, the creditors come calling.

Drug Effects on the Body

Addictionologist Douglas Talbott, M.D., estimates that about two out of five people who use psychoactive substances eventually become addicted to them. As the body adjusts to—that is, tolerates—the drug's effects through repeated intake, the user needs an increasing dosage to obtain the same intensity and duration of the original experience. Habitual users may never again reach the early highs. Instead, they find they must take more and more drugs just to avoid withdrawal symptoms, which range from flu-like problems to seizures or even death.

"There is one part of the brain that most drugs of abuse seem to affect," explains a neuroscientist.

Called the "brain reward system," it controls our feeling states and emotions. Drugs of abuse have the unique capacity to directly affect the brain reward system, bypassing the normal channels of information processing. When you take a drug and use it repeatedly, there are fundamental changes that happen in your brain and over time, those changes basically change the way you view the world (Video: National Institute on Drug Abuse, 1993).

Once a person becomes addicted, it is extremely difficult to change a drug-dependent lifestyle into one that is drug free. The brain, a malleable organ, changes structure and function according to life experiences. It is, one doctor says, ". . . constantly 'wiring' 're-wiring' and possibly 'unwiring' itself, forming and re-forming synapses between neurons" (Kotzsch, 1993, p. 160). Another physician compares the brain's synapses to a telephone company's circuitry. "The circuits still work after a long period of non-use. The 'lines' in our brain that were established by drugs are still there waiting for us after a long absence" (Coombs, 1997, p. 65).

Experiments performed in the 1950s asked this simple question while probing the brains of rats with a stimulating electrode: Will a rat exert effort in order to be electrically stimulated in a particular part of the brain? The researchers discovered that rats would indeed press a lever tens of thousands of times in succession, ignoring normal needs for food, water, and rest to gain electrical stimulation in certain regions of the brain. Electrical activation in these regions, called "the pleasure centers" or "brain reward regions," is profoundly reinforcing or addictive (Hyman, 1995).

Not surprisingly, drugs also stimulate the human brain, triggering the same kind of addiction. Chronic use causes long-lived molecular changes in the signaling properties of nerve cells (called neurons). "In particular," Dr. Hyman states, "drugs of abuse appear to commandeer circuits intimately involved in the control of emotion and motivation, thus impairing the insight and even the volition of the addicted person. At the same time, they produce nearly indelible emotional memories that predispose the person to drug craving and hence to relapse" (Hyman, 1995, p. 30).

Teens who experiment with drugs or use them socially don't plan to become addicted, of course. Unfortunately, drug users become less capable over time of making sound decisions about the situation. "Knowing that drugs of abuse commandeer key motivational circuits in the brain explains the otherwise irrational behavior of addicted people despite mounting evidence that they are killing themselves and alienating all who are most important to them in their lives" (Hyman, 1995, p. 33).

Sidebar 2.1: Deferring Gratification

Few four-year-olds are drug addicts, but most have a similar problem—lack of willpower. You can prove it with Oreo cookies. Sit a typical child of four at a table and offer a choice—one cookie right now, or two if the kid is willing to wait while the adult in charge leaves the room for a while. Usually, kids say they'd prefer to wait and get two cookies. So the adult leaves, but an Oreo remains on the table. Most kids cave in and go for the cookie—in less than a minute.

The capacity to defer gratification—and to exert better control over one's behavior—generally improves with age. Six-year-olds can wait for the adult to return. But drug addicts seem to exhibit the willpower of four-year-olds; the self-control of adulthood is utterly defeated by a chemical conspiracy inside their brains (Siegfriend, 2000).

Drug Effects on Emotional Development

As adolescents slide into deeper levels of drug use, they increasingly avoid more positive activities in favor of their drug habits. Not only do they lose the potential physical, intellectual, emotional, and spiritual benefits of positive activities, they replace them with an unhealthy activity that eventually undermines their life quality. And, each time they use drugs to fix uncomfortable feelings, they strengthen the habit and reinforce a vicious cycle.

Personal growth comes only through struggle. As bodybuilders say, "No pain, no gain." And as the mythical king who demanded a "royal road to geometry" (the ability to master it without studying) discovered, the only way to develop mentally is to struggle with intellectual problems. Giving math students the correct answers before they grapple with problems only impedes their potential intellectual growth.

It's the same way with emotions. If every time young people experience uncomfortable feelings they suppress them by using psychoactive drugs, they suspend their emotional growth. Like physical and mental muscle, "emotional muscle" develops only when we learn to tolerate emotional discomfort and wrestle with our problems. There is no "royal road" to emotional growth.

Sidebar 2.2: Emotional Impairment

"Drinking retarded my emotional development and growth as a person," a drug abuser reflected. "It retarded my growing up. In the last few years I have just begun to catch up" (Coombs, 1997, p. 93).

It may surprise you that many professionals entrusted with our safety and well-being also naively become addicted. In dozens of interviews with addicted physicians, dentists, nurses, pharmacists, airline pilots, and attorneys (Coombs, 1997), the licensed individuals recalled that psychoactive drugs at first made their lives better—more rewarding and fulfilling. Only later did they realize that, by bypassing problem-solving opportunities, they had also bypassed personal growth. "Alcohol had been a tranquilizer for my emotions and helped me deal with problems I was afraid to handle," one explained. "But it not only stopped fixing my emotional problems; it made them worse. I used alcohol as a coping mechanism" (Coombs, 1997, p. 93).

Thus emotional atrophy occurs when people learn to rely on drugs as a way to deal with uncomfortable feelings. If the drugs are discontinued, former users must return to where they left off in their emotional development—the age when they first started using drugs to cope—and begin growing from there. Thus a forty-five-year-old may have an emotional age of only fifteen. It's no wonder that so many addicts find it extremely difficult to discontinue using drugs, and if they do, they often relapse.

As a person ingests more and more drugs, over time the substances damage the brain's normal processes. Dependent on ingested chemicals, the part of the brain designed to produce chemicals creating normal emotions shuts down. When this happens, the addict needs more and more of the drug in order to feel adequate. As we discussed earlier, addicts rarely, if ever, achieve the highs they did during their first drug experiences. Just trying to feel normal now consumes their time and energy.

Once users become psychologically addicted to drugs as "problem-solvers," they cannot simply toss the drugs aside and walk away—because their coping skills have withered. It is terrifying for them to consider a day without drugs, and some even regard death as a better alternative. The user sees the drugs as a built-in entertainment center, therapist, and buddy, a virtual-reality world where dreams seem to come true. Of course, the drugs eventually stop serving in these roles and the user ultimately struggles merely to survive and feel normal.

Sidebar 2.3: Betrayed by "Best Friend"

"Alcohol, my best friend, turned on me. My best friend ended up grabbing me so that I couldn't give it up; I *had* to drink. I thought that it was a friend, but before I knew it I drank not because I wanted to, but because I *had* to; I could not *not* drink. I thought chemicals were my close companion and support, but they were killing me" (Coombs, 1997, p. 141).

Being asked to "work at living" again can deliver quite a shock to recovering users. Fred Zackon and his colleagues (1993) pointed out that everyone needs pleasure and that giving up drugs should not mean giving up fun. In fact, the person whose mind, body, and lifestyle are no longer addicted can have more fun in more ways than ever before. Most drug-free pleasures, however, require effort. With drugs it comes automatically: Take drugs—feel better. The now-passive user may not remember the time when he used to go hiking, plan, study, date, or converse without chemical assistance. "A person who has mainly relied on drugs for fun, and whose nervous system has been accustomed to very abnormal stimulation, has to readjust" (Zackon et al., 1993, p. 109).

In short, psychoactive drugs interfere with the normal process of growth. When kids use drugs to suppress shyness, loneliness, boredom, depression, and anxiety or to create feelings of euphoria, they bypass the development of the healthy coping skills they will need to handle problems throughout their lives. "A teenager on drugs does not grow emotionally," Meehan (1984, p. 53) emphasizes. "All that grows is the magnitude of his problems. That is why drugs are so devastating to young, unformed psyches. Exactly at the time when young people need to learn how to deal with adult problems, drugs give them a means of sidestepping those problems."

Sidebar 2.4: Good and Bad Habits

What is the difference between good and bad habits? Good habits (for example, exercising, taking classes, and saving money) are self-enhancing. Although they require effort up front, they yield positive long-term benefits. Bad ones, by contrast (for instance, gambling, adultery, debt-spending, and drug use), may be initially rewarding, but they invariably have negative consequences (Marlatt and Gordon, 1985).

Now let's take a look at the most popular mood-altering drugs and see how they can impair emotional development and health.

A C T I V I T I E S   F O R   P A R E N T S   A N D   K I D S

2.1 Ask your kids how drug use affects the people they know in both positive and negative ways.

smoking—positive/negative
alcohol—positive/negative
other drug substances—positive/negative

2.2 Ask your kids to describe the difference between good and bad habits. Then read the quote in Sidebar 2.4 and ask them if they agree or disagree with it. Think of more examples or discuss the long- and short-term benefits of the examples given.

2.3 Discuss what would happen to a baby if her mother carried her everywhere, even after she got old enough to walk. What if the mother anticipated all her needs so that she didn't need to talk? What if, when she went to school, her mother went with her and did her schoolwork for her, or just kept her home to "protect her"? In what ways could psychoactive drugs be like this mother?

REFERENCES

Coombs, Robert H. 1997. *Drug-Impaired Professionals.* Cambridge, MA: Harvard University Press.

Hyman, Steven E. 1995. "The Addicted Brain." *Harvard Medical Alumni Bulletin,* Winter, pp. 29–33.

Kotzsch, R. E. 1993. "Brain Fitness—Develop Your Powers of Mind." *Natural Health,* May–June, pp. 159–160.

Meehan, Bob. 1984. *Beyond the Yellow Brick Road: Our Children and Drugs.* Rockville Center, NY: Farnsworth Publishing Company.

Marlatt, G. Alan & Gordon, Judith R., Eds. 1985. *Relapse Prevention: Maintenance Strategies in the Treatment of Addictive Behaviors.* New York: Guilford Press.

National Institute on Drug Abuse. 1993. *Drug Abuse and the Brain.* NCADI Videotape Resource, No. 57. Rockville, MD: National Clearinghouse for Alcohol and Drug Information.

Siegfriend, Tom. 2000. "Pathways of Addiction . . . Drug Abuse Studies Focus on How Areas of the Brain Interact." Science Editor of the *Dallas Morning News* (reporting on scientific papers presented in San Francisco at the Annual Meeting of the Cognitive Neuroscience Society, April 17), Section F, pp. 1, 7.

Zackon, Fred, McAuliffe, William E., & Ch'ien, James M. N. 1993. *Recovery Training and Self-Help: Relapse Prevention and Aftercare for Drug Addicts.* National Institutes of Health 93-3521. Washington, DC: U.S. Department of Health and Human Services, Public Health Service.

PART TWO

What Should I Know About Drugs?

Psychoactive drugs—including alcohol and tobacco—affect both body and mind. Drug abuse is the inappropriate use of any substance that alters feelings or state of consciousness. "I would take anything that moved my mood," a drug abuser confessed. "I had a pharmacy of stuff that I used. I could recover from drinking the night before by using Empirin Three and Tylenol Three [both contain codeine]. They energized me, just like the crystal. It was an immediate love affair. But basically I was a beverage man."

As you read the following descriptions, keep in mind the difference between *physiological* addiction and *psychological* addiction. When a person is physically addicted, their body craves the drug and experiences unpleasant withdrawal symptoms such as nausea and chills without it. However, the mentally and emotionally addicted person uses drugs to cope with life's challenges. They believe they can't function without this "friend"—one that ultimately betrays. Psychological dependence is even more difficult to overcome than physical dependence.

3 Legal Drugs of Abuse

Most kids experiment with tobacco and alcohol. Because use of these substances usually precedes the use of illegal drugs, many experts refer to tobacco and alcohol (and sometimes marijuana) as "gateway drugs." Although society assumes that tobacco and alcohol are less dangerous than their illegal counterparts, research shows that the opposite is true.

Tobacco

About 4.5 million teenagers ages twelve through seventeen are smokers. Three thousand adolescents begin smoking each day, and one-third of them will eventually die from addiction-related problems (*Prevention Pipeline,* 1996). Adolescents use tobacco to feel "cool" and grown up. For many, smoking symbolizes independence and adulthood. Some girls use nicotine as an appetite suppressant. Kids fail to realize that cigarettes and other forms of tobacco are addictive and should be treated with the same caution as illegal street narcotics. "For me it is a social thing," said a fifteen-year-old. "My boyfriend smokes. I can quit any time I want because I'm strong, but I don't want to."

Sidebar 3.1: Cigarette News Release: Addiction Can Start Early

"Scientists have confirmed a suspicion held by some smokers but never proven: It could take just a few cigarettes to become addicted. Some 12- and 13-year-olds showed evidence of addiction within days of their first cigarette, according to research reported this week in the British Medical Association journal *Tobacco Control.* The study, conducted in 1998, followed 681 12- to 13-year-olds in central Massachusetts for a year and tracked their smoking habits. 'The really important implication of this study is that we have to warn kids that you can't just fool around with cigarettes or experiment with cigarettes for a few weeks and then give it up,' said Dr. Joseph DiFranza, who led the research at the University of

Massachusetts. 'If you fool around with cigarettes for a few weeks, you may be addicted for life'" (Ross, 2000).

Quitting is never as easy as one might first imagine. Although most smokers can temporarily stop—"No problem; I've quit a thousand times"— it's hard to *stay stopped*. Studies indicate that 75 to 80 percent of those addicted to nicotine would like to quit but have been unable to do so. (Less than 20 percent succeed in stopping on the first try.) The relapse rate of those who quit for the first time, like that of recovering alcoholics and heroin addicts, is strikingly high—about 75 percent.

Most teens who smoke want to stop. Nearly half of the high school seniors in the survey said they'd like to quit smoking. But they can't because, according to the Surgeon General's Report, "most young people who smoke daily are addicted to nicotine." In the same survey, about 40 percent said they tried to quit and couldn't (www.cdc.gov/tobacco/).

"I started at age sixteen and smoked up to two packs a day for twenty years," an ex-smoker recounts. "I quit for about ten months, and then decided to start again. Seventeen years later, I smoked my last cigarette. I averaged three packs per day at that time, sometimes up to four. I knew I was addicted, and I knew it was not good for me. I could tell because I easily ran out of breath. Last year they discovered cancer and the lower two lobes of my right lung were removed."

Sidebar 3.2: Tobacco Facts

One-third of the world's population over age fifteen are regular smokers. Because U.S. cigarette smoking is declining (only 4 percent of smokers worldwide), U.S. tobacco companies R.J. Reynolds and Phillip Morris sell more products in foreign than domestic markets. Worldwide, tobacco kills 3.5 million people annually. These deaths exceed those caused by AIDS, tuberculosis, auto accidents, homicide, and suicide combined. Worse, the death toll is expected to rise to 10 million by 2020, with 7 million in developing countries (Wolfe, 1998).

Cigarette smoke contains some four thousand chemicals, the most highly addictive of which is nicotine. Two hundred of the chemicals are known poisons (www.health.org/pubs). Like many drugs that affect the nervous system, nicotine at once stimulates and relaxes the body. Because it is inhaled, it reaches the brain in only seven to ten seconds—twice as fast as intravenous drugs do, and three times faster than alcohol. After a few puffs, the level of nicotine in the blood skyrockets. The smoker becomes more alert, can think faster, and feels calmer (because nicotine triggers the release of a natural opiate called beta-endorphin).

Sidebar 3.3: High-risk Behaviors

"By age 10 or 11 those kids who smoke are already making a commitment towards the social acceptability of smoking," reports Dr. McDermott of University of South Florida's College of Public Health. "Research has demonstrated adolescent smokers are more likely than nonsmokers to drink, experiment with drugs, engage in unsafe sex, carry weapons and become involved in other high-risk behaviors" (www.kidsource.com/index.html).

Not classified as an addicting drug by the Food and Drug Administration until 1996, tobacco may seem safe because it has been widely accepted—25 percent of all U.S. adults currently smoke. Nicotine doesn't cause hallucinations or pack the same euphoric punch as some other drugs. A crack user, for example, may overdose and die immediately. Nobody lights up a cigarette and dies on the spot, but problems eventually show up. Whereas cocaine kills no more than a thousand U.S. citizens annually, smoking kills about 418,000 of them each year. The World Health Organization estimates more than three million deaths from smoking worldwide. Moreover, secondhand smoke also harms the health of the user's family and friends (www.kickbutt.org/youth/factguide/13.html).

- "Secondhand smoke causes thirty times more lung-cancer deaths than all regulated pollutants combined.
- "Secondhand smoke kills about three thousand nonsmokers each year through lung cancer.
- "Secondhand smoke causes up to three hundred thousand lung infections (such as pneumonia and bronchitis) in infants and young children each year (www.cdc.gov/tobacco).

Alcohol

All alcoholic beverages—beer, wine, or distilled liquor—contain the same active chemical, ethanol. One ounce of distilled liquor contains the same amount of alcohol as an eight-ounce glass of wine or a twelve-ounce can of beer.

Sidebar 3.4: Alcohol, a Dangerous Drug

"If alcohol were a newly developed 'designer drug' just emerging from an underground chemist's lab, its intoxicating and addictive properties would lead to its scheduling under the Controlled Substances Act. As a carcinogen even at low doses, it could not be approved as a routine preventive medicine, and it has no current use in clinical medicine, so it would be classified in Schedule I: that is, completely banned except for tightly regulated research. Its recreational and social benefits would simply not enter into the decision" (Kleinman, 1992, p. 206).

Alcohol, the drug most widely used by young people, is rarely viewed by them as dangerous. "Drunk," "bombed," "smashed," "buzzed," or "wasted" are among the terms teens use to describe the effects of this legal, easily accessible, and relatively inexpensive drug. For people at any age, alcohol is a socially approved way to get "high" and to suppress anxieties. "Alcohol relieved my inhibitions and made me more outgoing," recalled an alcoholic about his teenage years. "I'd always been introverted and kept to myself, but alcohol relieved those feelings." "What alcohol did for me was allow me to escape, to get the hell out of there," another explained. "No matter where I was, I didn't have to be there."

Alcohol, a "downer," depresses the normal functioning of the central nervous system. Its effects depend on the quantity consumed; drinking rate; amount and kind of food in the drinker's stomach; and the size, tolerance, and emotional state of the drinker. One or two drinks usually reduce inhibitions, making conversation and emotional expression much easier. Three or four drinks taken in a short period of time cause flushing, dizziness, and poor coordination. Other symptoms of alcohol overuse (intoxication) include slurred speech, an unsteady walk, relaxed inhibitions, impaired coordination, and slowed reflexes. You can detect alcohol use by the smell of alcohol on the breath or clothes, intoxicated behavior, glazed eyes, and eventual hangover.

At the early stages of intoxication, alcohol blocks awareness of unpleasant events in a person's past or future. "I wanted to be out of the pain," a teen remarked. "I just wanted not to hurt. So I went straight to my parent's liquor cabinet, got the bottle of Grand Marnier and started drinking it." Alcohol also relaxes inhibitions and allows youngsters to party while feeling high. "At parties I learned how to take drugs and drink," recalled a young woman. "It really loosened up my inhibitions. It was a neat experience and I loved it."

At later stages of intoxication, the body tries to remove the chemical through vomiting. Repeated alcohol use can lead to dependence, and stopping suddenly causes withdrawal symptoms, such as severe anxiety, tremors, hallucinations, and convulsions. Even low doses significantly impair judgment and coordination, increasing the likelihood of auto and other accidents. Low to moderate use also increases the incidence of aggressive acts and impairs higher mental functioning, severely altering the person's ability to learn and remember information. Very high consumption causes depression and death.

If combined with other drugs that also depress the central nervous system, a smaller quantity of alcohol will produce pathological effects. When alcohol is ingested in combination with barbiturates or other depressant drugs, the "downer" effect is magnified and body functions can slow down so markedly that breathing may stop. Drinkers who also use marijuana may be unaware of the extent of their intoxication and think they can still drive safely. The combined effect of these drugs distorts timing and depth perception, and impairs judgment and coordination. If a person uses cocaine and alcohol together, the depressive effect of alcohol intensifies. As with marijuana, this combination can cause users, who now have reduced awareness of their level of intoxication, to become deluded and highly dangerous drivers.

Drinking (and other drug use) can also put teens in situations they no longer have the judgment, or even the consciousness, to control. One young woman who drank heavily at a party was held upside down by male companions on a diving board, while they dunked her repeatedly head-first into the swimming pool. After another party, a man who gave her a ride home raped her. Though drinking seemed glamorous, even liberating, to her before the party, she felt very differently about it the next morning. In retrospect, self-control can look a lot more like freedom: the freedom to make wise and healthy choices. (See Appendix A: How Are Alcohol and Other Drugs Affecting Your Life? A Self-Test for Teenagers.)

ACTIVITIES FOR PARENTS AND KIDS

3.1 Drinking may help people "loosen up," but does it really make them better conversationalists or company? Share personal experiences with your kids.

3.2 What does it mean to have fun? Share your "most fun" memories. Ask your kids whether they really "need" alcohol to have fun. Do adults?

3.3 Ask your kids why teenagers smoke. How can smoking be so popular in societies that emphasize health and fitness?

3.4 Discuss the difference between alcohol and illegal drugs. What makes drinking "okay" but other drugs "not okay"?

3.5 Many kids may ask why alcohol seems to be okay for adults but not for kids. Discuss your views on this.

REFERENCES

Kleinman, Mark. 1992. *Against Excess: Drug Policy for Results.* New York: Basic Books.
Prevention Pipeline. July/August, 1996.
Ross, Emma. 2000. "Cigarette Addiction Can Start Early." From: www.latimes.com/health/
    medicine, September 11.
Wolfe, Sidney M., Ed. 1998. *Health Letter,* October.

INTERNET SOURCES

www.kidsource.com/index.html. Quoting from Florida Health Information Center at the
    University of South Florida College of Public Health, March 18, 1996, 813-974-3300.
www.cdc.gov/tobacco/
www.kickbutt.org/youth/factguide/13.html
www.health.org/pubs

4 Illegal Drugs of Abuse

Kids' experimentation with drugs may escalate to illegal substances such as marijuana, cocaine and other stimulants, hallucinogens, depressants, narcotics, inhalants, anabolic steroids, and "designer" drugs.

Marijuana

Called "pot," "dope," "grass," "weed," or "maryjane," marijuana comprises 90 percent of illicit drug use. Nearly half of all teenagers experiment with marijuana (Rosenbaum, 1998, p. 198).

Dried marijuana leaves, seeds, and flowers look like dried parsley with stems and seeds. Usually smoked in a pipe or made into a cigarette called a "joint," pot exudes an odor of burned hemp rope. When ground up, this drug may be mixed with food such as cookies or brownies, or put into drinks. Marijuana paraphernalia include rolling papers, pipes, and roach clips (metal clamps used to hold the cigarette). The drug is generally sold in grams and stored in plastic sandwich bags; some people use other kinds of containers such as film canisters to store it.

The slow effects of marijuana on a teenager make its use difficult to detect. The drug has a half-life (the time it takes to go from full strength to half-strength in the body) of twenty-four to forty-eight hours. By contrast, alcohol has a half-life of three to four hours, and thus is eliminated much more quickly from the system. The potential for marijuana overdose is very low and can be detected only in a slow deterioration in performance over a period of several months.

Marijuana produces immediate, temporary changes in the user's thoughts, perceptions, and information processing. Studies also show that it affects short-term memory and comprehension and diminishes capacity to learn and recall new information. Automobile driving, which requires concentration and coordination, may deteriorate with marijuana use. A former marijuana user explains:

I'm in a demanding career where I'm frequently tested in a simulated performance situation that requires coordination of mind and body. I'm also
required to memorize lots of numbers and procedures. When I didn't perform
as well as the other guys, I thought I wasn't as smart as they were. I'd really get
frustrated, "Wow, how could I have missed that?" Now I realize I'm just as
smart and well coordinated as they are. My deficient performance was due to
my long-term pot use.

Marijuana cigarettes do not contain filters. Because users often inhale
the unfiltered smoke deeply and hold it in their lungs as long as possible,
marijuana can damage the lungs and pulmonary system. Smoking
marijuana (and crack cocaine) also causes the same kinds of precancerous
conditions—the same molecular changes—that result from smoking
cigarettes.

Habitual use of marijuana during adolescence can also diminish future
pleasures. "Kids who use marijuana heavily in their early years in connection with enjoyable activities such as sex," noted one research professor,
"generally don't enjoy those same pleasurable activities later on without
marijuana." Even simple pleasures may be dulled by pot. "I couldn't go to
the beach without getting high first," a long-term user confessed. "I couldn't
have a good time without it."

Some users contend that marijuana is not addictive. "I personally find
that assertion humorous," said an ex-user who had smoked pot from ages
fourteen to thirty-six,

> because I *was* addicted—maybe not physically, but certainly psychologically.
> Marijuana was my vehicle for altering my mood and feeling. At first, it was my
> companion, my loyal friend that helped me to relax, unwind, and take the
> edge off. But then it became a necessity. I couldn't go to the supermarket with-
> out getting high first. I needed it just to feel normal.

Sidebar 4.1: Wonder Drug

"I smoked marijuana every single day for twenty-three years and
viewed it as a wonder drug because it took away my fears and anxieties
about socializing. I had always been timid and afraid in a crowd and
couldn't connect with people, especially women. It was hard for me to
go to dances, all the things that normal kids do. But with marijuana, I
suddenly felt relaxed and sociable, a way to be happy. This led to the use
of many other drugs, an attempted suicide, and drug treatment. I now
realize that the first day I used marijuana to cope was the day I stopped

growing emotionally and socially. I've had to learn all over again how to socialize and live life like regular people. And I'm still learning; it's not over!"

Because marijuana use is illegal, users risk incarceration. Under our present laws, many otherwise law-abiding citizens serve prison time for possession of marijuana. Advice? "Educate your kids before they start using it," replied an ex-user. "Tell them there are lots of people out there who want you to try it with them, saying it's fun and a good time. Tell them that you're not missing anything. These people aren't your friends."

Sidebar 4.2: Experiencing Life Naturally

People stoned on marijuana tend to focus on one thing at a time: the food, the music, the dog. Conversation deteriorates. More important, says professor Steve Succman, "You don't learn how to cope with real life. You don't learn how to experience life in real terms, to feel bad *normally*. Let's say you smoked marijuana heavily from age 16 to 26, then stopped. The way you process life events emotionally after that may be more like a 16-year-old" (Morrow, 1996, p. 30).

Cocaine

Users typically ingest cocaine, a white crystalline powder derived from the South American coca plant, by "snorting" it into the nose through a small glass tube or straw. This highly addictive, powerful stimulant often comes diluted with other ingredients. Users employ razor blades to divide the powder into "lines," or snort-sized portions.

Users can also inject cocaine intravenously or smoke it in its "freebase" or "crack" form; in either case, the high occurs within seconds. Crack looks like small lumps or soap shavings with a porcelain texture and often comes packaged in small vials. It makes a crackling sound (hence its name) when it is heated, owing to the baking soda used in its preparation.

In any form, cocaine stimulates the central nervous system and provides a peak experience in a short time. A sudden drop-off in mood (the "crash") occurs as the drug wears off. The drug produces a tremendous craving for the high, and the crash that follows only intensifies the need to find and use more.

Sidebar 4.3: Obsession With a Drug

"Cocaine blocks out everything, but you don't care. I look back now in despair and see how cocaine, little by little, took precedence over everything in my life, including food. Unlike other drugs, the cocaine high is so strong that everything else is of little importance, and you are obsessed with that euphoric pleasure that you felt last time."

Cocaine directly stimulates the pleasure center of the brain. It delivers such an impact that users can forget their own names. For some, the drug seems to provide a solution to all their problems, and soon dominates all aspects of life. "Bingo!" exclaimed one user, "It made me witty, gave me lots of energy, and I was sure it enhanced my personality. All my friends did it. We thought it was a harmless social thing we could handle."

Cocaine addiction erodes users' physical and mental health, impairs schoolwork and careers, jeopardizes relationships with family and friends, and drains financial resources. Some users, spending hundreds or thousands of dollars on cocaine and crack each week, will do anything to support their habit. Many turn to selling drugs, prostituting themselves, or committing other crimes. Cocaine and crack have played a role in a number of drownings, car crashes, falls, burns, and suicides. Moreover, these drugs carry a serious potential for overdose, because it is difficult to control the amount absorbed in the bloodstream.

Other Stimulants

Like cocaine, amphetamines, methamphetamine, and other stimulants excite the central nervous system, producing intense feelings of alertness and energy. Usually taken orally, these drugs are sometimes called "speed," "uppers," "crank," and "ice." In most cases, they produce a high that lasts two to four hours, followed by an unpleasant crash. Some users report a feeling of relaxation and emotional openness. In this state, problems seem to disappear, and users feel receptive to those around them, self-assured, friendly, and sociable.

Stimulants, commonly advertised in college newspapers during exam time, are widely used on university campuses by students who are desperate to stay awake. "In dental school I was introduced to amphetamines to stay awake and study," a student confessed. "I used to stay awake by making my way through three to four liter bottles of cola." One informal conversation among ten classmates revealed that seven had used stimulants to study longer during final exams. They had used them to study until about four o'clock in the morning, then they took a sleeping pill to get a few hours of sleep before the exam.

Depressants

Depressant drugs (barbiturates, benzodiazepines, and tranquilizers) usually come in the form of red, yellow, blue, or red/blue capsules called "downers," "tranks," "ludes," "reds," or "yellow jackets." Like alcohol, these drugs bring one's mood and energy level down. "I went berserk on Valium," said a user. "I thought those pills were the greatest thing that had ever happened."

Small amounts of any depressant can produce calmness and relax muscles, but larger doses can cause slurred speech, a staggered gait, and altered perception. Extremely large doses can bring respiratory depression, coma, and even death. Alcohol multiplies the effects of the drugs and therefore compounds their risks.

With depressants, teenagers mainly seek to feel relaxed, "mellow," and free from everyday worries and cares. Depressants also mask inhibitions and anxieties, letting users act gregarious and spontaneous at social gatherings.

Hallucinogens

Hallucinogenic drugs distort the senses, making users "see" smells and "hear" colors, and causing inanimate objects to seem animated. Sights and sounds may merge and intensify, and one's sense of time may be altered. Wanting to experience something more beautiful and intense than the ordinary, users may achieve what feels like a transcendent or spiritual state or a sense of enhanced creativity. "I made friends with the guys next door," a user recalled. "We tried psychedelic mushrooms. We got a kick out of them and really enjoyed all the visuals."

Sometimes "bad trips" may occur—frightening hallucinations, loss of personal boundaries, and terrifying perceptual changes. A bad trip can cause paranoid feelings, extreme anxiety, and sometimes panic. Users never know when such an experience will strike, and some victims require psychiatric hospitalization.

LSD, called "acid," is the major drug in this category. It comes in brightly colored tablets, which users take orally. A typical acid trip lasts between two and twelve hours, and can significantly impair brain function (hence the use of the word "fried" to describe long-time users). LSD users may also experience occasional frightening "flashbacks"—spontaneous recurrences of the LSD experience without actual use of the drug. Flashbacks can be deadly, especially if they strike while the victim is driving or engaging in some other activity that requires clear thinking and skill.

Sidebar 4.4: LSD Use: Just Another Life Experience?

One young woman had a friend who had used a lot of pot and tried acid, with no apparent ill effects. She recalled an argument with him about the dangers of his LSD use. "He kept saying acid was just another life experience, an adventure. Finally, I asked him, 'If you were a parent, would you let your child use it?' He shut up really fast, and then shook his head. End of story."

Other hallucinogens—PCP, a liquid taken orally; and mushrooms ("shrooms"), dried and then eaten—have an LSD-like effect as well.

Narcotics

Narcotics (opiates) are the most effective pain relievers physicians have. They can also stimulate the pleasure centers of the brain, or act on the respiratory center in the brainstem, slowing or shutting it down. The short-term effect of a smaller dose is a state of contentment, detachment from concern, and freedom from distressing emotions. "When I used codeine," a nurse explained, "I could do my job better and accomplish more. It made it easy to talk with people. It was the magic cure—*the* cure!"

A larger dose causes euphoria and a heightened sense of well-being. "The doctor prescribed Vicoden for headache," reported one user. "The damn things would sing to me from the drawer!" (Coombs, 1997, p. 129). A moderately large dose impairs mental and physical activity. The body feels warm, the extremities heavy, and the mouth dry. Sleep follows.

Opiates come in different colored capsules, tablets, syrups, and suppositories. Morphine and codeine, available in many widely used prescription medicines, also come in synthetic form—meperidine and methadone, respectively.

Once dependent on these drugs, addicts will do outrageous things to get them, as this emergency-room nurse reports. "Once I did intravenous morphine, I was gone! I wanted it again and again: Give it to me quick! After experiencing this, I began stealing my patients' drugs."

Opiates induce rapid, powerful physical and psychological dependence, because constantly larger doses are required to produce the same effect. Withdrawal from these drugs causes severe physical reactions—

nervousness, anxiety, sleeplessness, runny nose and eyes, sweating, muscle twitching, severe aching of the back and legs, hot and cold flashes, vomiting, and diarrhea.

Some experts consider codeine-derived prescription pain killers (such as Percoset and Percodan) the hardest of hard-core drugs. These medications usually come in pill form, work as depressants, and remove feelings of pain from the mind. They have a high potential for overdose and are dangerous when combined with other drugs. If you keep prescription pain killers at home, keep them locked up. Make them available to your kids only under the supervision of an addiction-savvy physician.

Heroin, called "junk" or "smack," is another powerful opiate. A white to dark-brown powder, it is usually dissolved in water and injected. Derived from opium, it causes quick, physical addiction. Most parents find it hard to believe that their teen could have access to heroin. ("Not *my* child!") Unfortunately, however, it happens. A grieving mother whose eighteen-year-old daughter died of a heroin overdose reports,

> About three weeks ago, before Tish died, she started hanging around a different group of people. She had broken up with her boyfriend and started staying out later than usual. She had always been a perfect kid. I thought she was too smart to get involved with drugs. She was my perfect Tish.

At the hospital, Tish's mom remembers hearing only the words "heroin," "brain-dead," and "drug overdose." "I always thought of heroin addicts as people on the streets with no home and dirty bodies, with track marks up and down their arms," she said. "I didn't realize that today's heroin is so strong, the purity level so high and that kids don't need to stick needles in their bodies. They can smoke it" (Video: *Heroin's Young Addicts*, 1996, p. 15 of transcript).

Inhalants

An inhalant is any gaseous substance drawn into the lungs. It gets absorbed into the bloodstream, where the gas takes the place of oxygen. As the brain becomes oxygen starved, the user begins to feel light-headed and experiences effects similar to those of depressants. Inhalant chemicals abused by teenagers include glue, gasoline, paint, hair sprays, and even the aerosol from whipped-cream cans.

Deep inhalation of these vapors, or the use of large amounts in a short time, can cause disorientation, violent behavior, unconsciousness, and death. Repeated, long-term use can permanently damage the nervous system, as cells starved for oxygen die. Youths who cannot afford more expensive drugs may turn to inhalants.

Anabolic Steroids

These drugs, powerful compounds closely related to the male sex hormone testosterone, are not mood-altering in the technical sense. But some young people use them inappropriately.

Because these substances build muscle mass quickly, young people may take them to enhance their appearance and athletic prowess. But in doing so, teens subject themselves to at least seventy side effects ranging in severity from acne to liver cancer. Male users have experienced withered testicles, sterility, and impotence. Females can develop irreversible masculine traits, breast reduction, and sterility. Psychological effects include aggressive behavior and depression. Some side effects appear quickly; others may not show up for years.

Designer Drugs

Because illegal drugs are defined by their chemical makeup, unscrupulous chemists can circumvent legal restrictions by modifying the molecular structure of certain illegal drugs. These analogues can prove several hundred times stronger than the substance they are designed to imitate, and can produce severe brain damage. Like amphetamines, many designer drugs have mild stimulant properties, but most are euphoriants (such as Ecstasy).

Some of these substances present an immediate physical and psychological threat to your child. And new ones are constantly cropping up. As a parent, you may feel that protecting your teens from these drugs is an overwhelming task. However difficult the challenge, make every effort. At stake is the well-being of your entire family.

ACTIVITIES FOR PARENTS AND KIDS

4.1 Ask your kids to list the illegal drugs they know about. Read about their effects together and discuss why kids might seek out these drugs.

4.2 Discuss the impact of "scare tactics" on teens. Does knowing that some users may *not* experience the worst effects of these drugs make trying them seem like a fair risk? In your kids' opinion, which possible effects are most worrisome?

4.3 Some people say that using drugs is liberating; others argue that true freedom is being able to make choices from a position of conscious self-control. Discuss this issue as a family, citing examples to support your points.

4.4 The U.S. government spends billions of dollars every year on "the War on Drugs," but the problem just keeps worsening. If you were appointed the nation's "drug czar," what would you do?

4.5 Visit the following Web sites and discuss what you learned. The Substance Abuse & Mental Health Services Administration (SAMHSA) (www.samhsa. gov) is a rich source of information from the federal government. National Clearinghouse for Alcohol & Drug Information (NCADI) (www.health.org) is another excellent source. Go to "related links" in this source to find an alphabetical listing of seventeen additional, major sites that will link you to more resources.

REFERENCES

Coombs, Robert H. 1997. *Drug-Impaired Professionals.* Cambridge, MA: Harvard University Press, p. 129.
Morrow, Lance. 1996. "Kids on Pot." *Time,* December 9, pp. 26–30.
Rosenbaum, Marsha. 1998. "'Just Say No' to Teenagers and Marijuana." *Journal of Psychoactive Drugs.* Vol. 30(2), April–June, p. 198.
Video. "Heroin's Young Addicts." 1996. *Oprah,* September 23. Chicago: Harpo Productions, p. 15 of transcript.

INTERNET SOURCES

www.health.org/reality/realitybytes/tenthings
www.health.org
www.samhsa.gov

PART THREE

How Do Kids Escalate in Drug Involvement?

Many kids get involved with drugs quite innocently and then gravitate toward deeper involvements until they jeopardize their health and well-being. They, like all of us, fit somewhere on this scale of drug involvement:

- *abstainers*—who don't use alcohol or other mind-altering drugs, about one–third of the American population.
- *social users*—who use substances in social situations.
- *drug abusers*—who get together with friends primarily to drink and/or use other drugs, and whose drug use gradually takes priority over other activities.
- *physically but not psychologically addicted users*—who can "walk away" from drugs after enduring physical withdrawal. Although these addicts gain psychological rewards from drugs, once they recognize that drugs create more problems than benefits, they can quit without a lot of help from others. Because they have developed emotional coping skills before using drugs, they are able to stay drug-free without relapsing.
- *psychologically dependent users*—who need mood-altering drugs to feel "normal" and to cope with daily living. Quitting drugs by will power alone is beyond their capability. "I knew I couldn't quit without help," one said. "I knew I couldn't make it through the weekend without getting drunk or loaded. I just couldn't do it. When others pressed me to stop I said, 'I just can't do this! Don't you understand?'"

The drug addict's lifestyle evolves through a series of stages: initiation, escalation, maintenance, discontinuation followed by relapse, and, for some, recovery. As a person progresses through the first three stages, commitment to drugs deepens along with the threat to a conventional lifestyle.

A drug user doesn't travel the course alone. Unwittingly or unwillingly, family members play a part. Chapters 5 and 6 trace the sequence of this journey, with a focus on family involvement at each stage.

5 Pre-Addiction Stages

Before becoming addicted, drug users proceed through two stages—initiation and escalation. Initiation does not mean the first time a teen tries a drug. It refers to the period when he or she uses drugs only occasionally. Escalation is a transitional time, when users start taking drugs more frequently, become interested in experimenting with different drugs, and spend more time with other users.

Initiation

During adolescence, young people have a number of developmental needs—independence from parents, adventure, and peer approval among them. Sadly, many parents do not realize how strong these needs are—and thus do nothing to help their kids meet them. As a result, some teens turn to drugs.

The Need for Independence

In the United States, there are no clear rites of passage to mark the shift from childhood to adulthood. Thus children must gradually gain for themselves the privileges of adult status. Achieving freedom and autonomy rarely comes easily, especially when parents use force as their primary method of managing their kids.

Force provides only a short-term means of control. It may work when parents are physically larger than their children, but it stops working as kids grow older. When parental demands compete with teens' need for independence, home can become a battleground. And as youths spend less time at home, parental influence weakens. Frustrated parents usually respond with criticism and threats of punishment. Such antagonism only alienates children—who react by spending even more time away from home. Increasingly, these adolescents meet needs for dignity, independence, and approval through their peers, widening the rift with parents and increasing the risk of drug use. The process accelerates when discouraged parents simply give up trying to influence their teens.

The Need for Adventure

Many teens experiment with drugs out of simple curiosity. Drugs, their illegal aspects, and potential dangers offer adventure, risk, challenge, and excitement—universal attractions for adolescents. Note the bravado in this teen, who, arrested for the first time, couldn't wait to tell his friends. "That's part of the whole joyous feeling," he said. "I just knew all my friends would say, 'Hey, man, what did you get busted for? All *right!* Did they beat you up? What happened?'" (Coombs & Coombs, 1988, p. 76).

Efforts to scare young people about the hazards of drugs are usually ineffective, if not counterproductive, because they unwittingly reinforce teens' desire for adventure. Outwitting the police, an extension of the games children play (cops and robbers, hide-and-seek, etc.) offers considerable excitement.

The Need for Peer Approval

The worst pain a teen can experience comes from being socially excluded from or ostracized by peers. The need for peer approval accounts for kids' rigid conformity to teen fashions and behaviors as they try to fit in, be "cool," and not stand out as different.

In adolescent gatherings, it is a rare teen who doesn't use alcohol and other drugs when friends are using them. "Alcohol helped me feel that I'm a gregarious girl," one said, "the life of the party and the center of the action." "When I started drinking," another explained, "it made me feel like one of the group. I thought I could dance and be more sociable. It changed me from an introvert to an extrovert, one of the gang."

A teenager's circle of friends is critical at this stage because these peers determine acceptable behaviors for members of the group. Once established, peer standards exert a powerful influence. This is why peer pressure is referred to as the "Pied Piper" of adolescence.

Not surprisingly, drug use is strongly connected to choice of friends. Kids who use alcohol and other drugs spend time with those who also use them. "In high school I hung around with people with the same interests, all the guys who enjoyed drinking," an addict recalled. "It was something I enjoyed, and we had lots of fun." Some groups can't even imagine a leisure activity that doesn't include alcohol. And users typically regard teens who don't use drugs or alcohol as "uncool."

Sidebar 5.1: Peer Pressure

Thirty percent of children in grades four through six report receiving "a lot" of pressure from their classmates to drink beer; 31 percent, to try marijuana; and 34 percent, to try cigarettes (*The Weekly Reader National Survey on Drugs and Alcohol*, 1995).

Positive family interactions at this stage can significantly diminish the risk of teen drug use. Kids from strong homes still need adventure and peer acceptance; however, they value their parents' opinions enough to select friends like themselves who don't use drugs. "If your friends don't use," a high school cheerleader explained, "it never comes up."

In contrast, kids who escalate into higher levels of drug use often describe their home life as emotionally unrewarding. Parents who give little time and attention to their children, who demonstrate little love and affection during their formative years, find that their influence erodes markedly during their kids' critical teenage years.

When parent-teen interaction is mostly negative communication— more arguing than listening, more criticism than praise, more frowning than smiling, more isolation than time together—youth turn to peers for what is lacking at home. "They never really showed me much love and affection," an addict recalled.

> My father never used to take me anywhere. I would be in Little League or something, and everybody's parents would come and watch, but mine never came. I didn't want to face it. I would hide it and I'd make excuses for them. I was always on the run, doing things with my friends. I would hide behind my drums out in the garage—isolated. I never came in except to eat and sleep (Coombs & Coombs, 1988, p. 79).

Sidebar 5.2: Alcohol-Related Accidents

Alcohol-related accidents are the leading cause of death among young people fifteen to twenty-four years of age. About half of all youthful deaths in drowning, fires, suicide, and homicide are alcohol related (*Growing Up Drug Free: A Parent's Guide to Prevention*, from www.health. org/pubs/parguide).

Escalation

Because most adolescents experiment with alcohol and marijuana, the critical question is, why do some teens escalate into a lifestyle in which alcohol and other drugs become their main focus? "It started off as an occasional drink at parties," one recalled. "Everybody does that. But later on it got worse and worse and worse."

Tolerance of drugs—physical dependence—does not develop with occasional use, but only when drugging becomes habitual. At that point, the user experiences withdrawal symptoms such as nausea, shaking, vomiting, and diarrhea when he or she stops taking the drug. When the addict uses the drug again, these symptoms go away.

How does a person get into such a sorry state? The escalation stage can be described as an apprenticeship period. During this time, teens prove themselves with drug-abusing peer groups, gaining experience and acceptance by established drug users. They learn how to use drugs and prove their loyalty to others who use. "Ask any drug user if his whole life has been miserable," a young adult challenged,

> and he will say that is not the case; he will tell you that drugs fit him well and that he likes the whole thing. When you get into drugs you have a good time. There are lots of rewards on the way up—involvement in a social group, status and acceptance by others, and a lot of recognition. If you are successful, people start to admire you just like they do in any group (Coombs & Coombs, 1988, p. 81).

During the escalation period, the user typically experiments with a variety of drugs. "I tried most every kind of pharmaceutical," one recalled, "every class of drug available; it was just curiosity. Then it became a matter of cutting ties with straight associates and spending more and more time on the streets." "It was a very progressive development," an alcoholic explains. "Looking back, about two years passed between the time alcohol was not an influence in my life to where it overcame all other activities."

Teens who escalate their drug use are not more peer-oriented than other kids. Their *selection of friends* distinguishes them. "I surrounded myself with people who did drugs," one noted. "All my friends were drinkers."

While new users consider substances secondary to their social activities—just one of the things they do at parties—drug abusers at the escalation stage plan their social life *around* alcohol and other drugs. Their drug use defines the group's purpose. "Every night we would go drink beer," an alcoholic remembered. "That's just what normal folks did, I thought. Nobody ever debated it or talked about whether it was a good or bad idea. In my circle of friends it was the normal lifestyle."

Despite sometimes outrageous behaviors at drug parties, escalating users regard these gatherings as fun, regardless of the consequences. "I guzzled some warm port wine and vomited all over the furniture in my friend's house," one recalled. "I also said some obscene things that made people laugh—I was quite the show. The next day as I was nursing a hangover, my friends stopped by and told me what a great time they had. I liked all the attention it gave me—so I was on my way with booze."

Sidebar 5.3: A Macho Thing

"To be a man, you've got to be a successful competitor." Drinking games, such as those notorious to fraternity parties, then become "the object to prove 'what a man I am,' because I can beat you. I can get drunker than you. I can down three six-packs." Fraternity men tend to hold the attitude, "I can drink more than you and not pass out. It's a macho thing," noted the director of the health-education unit of the UCLA Student Health Service (Elmore, 1997, p. 3).

During the escalation stage, the drug user's family also goes through predictable experiences. At first parents are usually unaware of the problem, especially if they don't have a close relationship with their teen. The typical family pattern at the time of escalation is one of little meaningful interaction. Parents may be busy with work and other concerns. In many such families, the father is a vague presence. In these cases, escalating teenagers spend less and less time at home and regard their parents primarily as providers of food and shelter. Friends now supply most of their much-needed emotional support. Increasingly, so do drugs or alcohol, which eventually replace friends. It becomes easier and easier for escalating teens to find a reason to use.

As early evidence of their child's substance use crops up, parents usually react with denial. "I don't know if they knew or if they just didn't want to accept the fact that their son might be smoking joints," mused a teenage boy. But eventually unmistakable evidence shows up and parents can no longer avoid the issue (Coombs & Coombs, 1988, p. 84).

Once they accept the fact their teen is using drugs, some parents try to save face by covering up the problem. For example, if their son is arrested for a minor offense, they bail him out as quickly and as quietly as possible. They may not take teenage drinking seriously, particularly in its early stages. However, as parents continue to see the unpleasant reality of their child's drinking or drug use, confrontations erupt. Ironically, this may be the most attention such parents have given their teen in years.

But no matter how good a parent you are, your kids may still use drugs. One mother, for example, made every effort to be loving and close to her three sons. Two gave her only minor problems, but her third son became involved in drugs.

He reeked of cigarette smoke and I found matches in his dirty laundry. I suspected he was also using alcohol and other drugs, so I leveled with him about my concerns and told him if push came to shove I would ship him off someplace away from his drug-using friends. He said his friends weren't bad people, they just did bad things. I talked to his brothers, hoping they could influence him, but they said, "Mom, there's not much you can do until he wants to change." One evening as my husband and I were watching TV, he came home, sat down, and stared at the wall. I asked him if something was wrong. After a while he said, "I need to talk," so we turned off the television. "I'm having a problem with drugs and I'm experiencing flashbacks and I'm scared to death," he said. "I'm afraid to go to class." [That's where his drug-using peers were.] We went to our family doctor and my son asked me to come in with him. It was hard to sit there and hear him admit to smoking pot, taking LSD, and drinking beer and hard liquor. I gasped, but I'll have to hand it to him for talking so openly in front of me. It showed me he really wanted help. The next day I made arrangements for him to transfer to another school away from his drug-using friends. I went with him to check out of his classes, and three of his six teachers wanted to know why. When I told them, they all said—in front of him—that he was a good kid and they were glad he asked for help. That was ten years ago, a turning point for him and, as far as I know, he has stayed clean ever since.

The social forces that encourage the drug-using lifestyle are everywhere—in the media, at school, at social events, and on the streets. Parents face a formidable task when they try to change the direction their child is headed.

Sidebar 5.4: Beer-Drinking Games

Three college graduates compiled a book of drinking games. The book talks not about the education they received in class, but about the "priceless" education they acquired while partying after, and according to them, before class. Drinking alcohol at a party, the authors argue, can teach students more about themselves than they can learn during four years in college.

The book contains more than sixty games. "Tang," invented by a group of students at Yale, is one of the more interesting activities. Players from two teams line up along the sides of a picnic table and rest their chins along the table's edge. Each player receives a full glass of beer, and the teams must chug them one at a time, in consecutive order. The first team to drink all the beer wins.

Each game comes with an illustration that the authors humorously connect to the game. Additionally, quotes from various well-known books and authors are strewn throughout the text to encourage drunkenness (McGuire, 1999).

ACTIVITIES FOR PARENTS AND KIDS

5.1 Discuss how fickle popularity is. For instance, think of people who were popular a year or two ago (or ten or twenty years!) and who aren't anymore. Also, discuss fads and fashions, joking about the styles that were "in" when you were younger. As a family, predict which fashions will be "in" five or ten years from now, and save your predictions to read when the time comes!

5.2 Role-play saying "no" in a "cool" way. Let your kids come up with the situations, and brainstorm responses together. Also, discuss how to avoid drug-related problem situations, and come up with an emergency escape plan in case your kids need one.

5.3 Kids often get into drugs while seeking independence, peer approval, and adventure. As a family, brainstorm ways kids can meet these needs without using drugs or alcohol.

REFERENCES

Coombs, Robert H., & Kathryn Coombs. 1988. "Developmental Stages in Drug Use: Changing Family Involvements." In *The Family Context of Adolescent Drug Use,* Ed. Robert H. Coombs. New York: The Haworth Press, pp. 73–98.

Elmore, Allison. 1997. "Beer and a Bong: Substance Abuse at UCLA." *UCLA Daily Bruin,* March 4, p. 3.

Growing Up Drug Free: A Parent's Guide to Prevention. U.S. Department of Education Catalogue #PHD533 from www.health.org/pubs/parguide.

McGuire, Barbara. 1999. "Bible of Beer-Drinking Games Entertains, Educates Partyers." *UCLA Daily Bruin,* November 29, pp. 23, 25–26.

The Weekly Reader National Survey on Drugs and Alcohol. Spring, 1995. Middletown, CT: Field Publications.

6 Addiction Stages

Once someone becomes addicted to drugs, everything else in life becomes secondary. In the *maintenance* stage, addicts use alcohol and other drugs not just for recreation but to get through the day. The length of time that users stay in this stage can vary from a few months to several decades. When the downward spiral of loss and conflict takes its inevitable toll, some addicts *discontinue* using drugs. Unfortunately, many relapse. However, some eventually become drug free, entering the *recovery* stage.

Maintenance

If teens escalate to the point of daily drug use, they reach the maintenance stage of physical and/or psychological addiction. In this stage, they become totally preoccupied with drugs. "Alcohol used to be my hobby," one said. "But as time went on, it became my sole recreation; this is when I became a maintenance drinker." Users now spend most of their time and energy getting and consuming drugs. "[They] devote their entire lives to that way of living," an addict explained. "Getting drugs is a daily obsession, a total devotion" (Coombs & Coombs, 1988, p. 85).

Sidebar 6.1: Rationalizations for Using Mood-Altering Drugs

Drug abusers find all kinds of reasons to use drugs, such as fatigue ("I need a pep pill"), emotional stress ("I need a tranquilizer"), physical pain or headaches ("I need pain-relief medication"), daily work ("I deserve a drink"), and achievement ("Let's celebrate").

Before the maintenance stage, it was "fun" for the young user to try different drugs, meet new friends, exchange information, and share experiences. Now, however, the pursuit of drugs takes on a desperate quality.

"My life was a mess," one addict recalled, "and everything seemed like it was such a struggle."

> You've got to fight to get to the top; and when you're there, you've got to maintain yourself in all areas, making sure that you have enough money to purchase your next supply, that you have a place to stay and can keep up with whatever material possessions you own, that those people who are fronting drugs or dealing for you are doing what they're supposed to. But whether you are on top or at the bottom, you are acutely aware that you have to maintain your existence at whatever point you are at (Coombs & Coombs, 1988, p. 85).

The maintenance stage brings new restrictions. At the initiation stage (Chapter 5), teens have a choice about going for a hamburger with one group of friends or using drugs with another. Because they still have social ties in both worlds, they can choose between two kinds of activities, both of which may seem pleasurable. At the escalation stage (Chapter 5), most users' friends are taking drugs, while still maintaining some ties to the "straight" world. If these young people are short on cash, they do not have to choose between eating or using drugs; they can do both, usually by borrowing from friends. At this stage, friends look after one another. Once they reach the maintenance stage, however, users can't count on borrowing money, because the other users they know are probably in the same predicament.

Sidebar 6.2: Managing Feelings

Managing feelings with chemicals can become an obsession. "My first addiction drove me to change my mood," one addict explained. "If I was in the same mood for an hour, it was time to change it. I tried everything."

In general, teenage friendship groups play two important roles: *instrumental* functions (helping one another to obtain money or drugs) and *expressive* functions (providing social and emotional rewards such as acceptance and support). At the initiation and escalation stages of drug use, friends typically fulfill both needs. But at the maintenance stage, peers serve mostly instrumental functions. In other words, the young addict looks at her "friends" and wonders, "How can these people help me get more drugs?" (As we will see later, users in the maintenance stage also regard family members as instrumental.)

With this new attitude, kids start moving from one group to another according to their survival instincts. And because they are sometimes pressured by the police and undercover narcotic agents, considerable suspicion arises within these fluid groups. One addict observed, "There is a lot of uptightness and lack of trust about who is a snitch." Psychological addiction becomes more likely and more powerful at this time, as self-serving relationships and shifting loyalties replace emotionally supportive friendships. Only the drug itself seems "reliable" and "supportive."

Of course, not all addicts are alike. Some—the stereotypical ones we usually read about in the newspapers—survive on the streets in "drug careers." Dropouts from conventional society—school and regular jobs—they live in an underground world focused on drug acquisition, use, and distribution. Politicians and police officers define them as America's drug problem and marshal enormous financial resources to catch and imprison them. However, these addicts are just a part of the problem.

Other addicts are ordinary folks, people we all know, even professionals we admire—doctors, dentists, pharmacists, nurses, pilots, or attorneys. Many of them begin using drugs for recreation or as "crutches" to help them function normally (Coombs, 1997). These addicts can go undetected much longer, because they have prestigious careers. Their families and co-workers cover up for them, and they have enough financial resources to obtain their drug supply.

Sidebar 6.3: A Poor Bargain

"I have a close friend, a former roommate who just got out of a drug-rehab center," said a college student. "I saw what drugs did to him. He was doing them every day and would come out of the bathroom all wired and antsy. He couldn't sleep at night. I saw his priorities shift away from school work to how many highs he could get in a day. Finally he was kicked out of school because he couldn't keep up. It changed his whole life!" (Coombs & Coombs, 1996, p. 88)

Drug users at this stage rarely live at home consistently with their parents. They typically "float in and out," more "in" during the escalation stage and more "out" during the maintenance stage. On impulse they may depart with little or no warning, leaving confused parents behind.

Drug-related activities only worsen any conflict and strain between users and their families. "Parents are in a bind and don't know what to do," a young addict noted. "On the one hand they don't want to put up with the behavior, yet they realize that it's their son or daughter and hope that things might change." But as the drug use progresses, parents' unrealistic hopes for change fade and their hurt and frustration increase.

At this stage, users consider their home only in utilitarian terms, as they manipulate their parents for money and other resources. When all else fails, addicts fall back on their families. If your kids are in this stage of drug use, try to remember that manipulation is the addict's chief survival skill. Teens do not necessarily use it with hurtful intent, but out of a desperate need for drugs. "Whenever I get released," a frequently arrested user explained, "I always play it to my people [his parents]. So I go home for a few hours and then go right back on the streets again." When parents resist providing more cash, their addicted children may "burn them." "I'd burglarize their house, and when they found out that I did, I told them they could buy the stuff back" (Coombs & Coombs, 1988, p. 90).

Some parents are so protective that they provide their addicted youngsters with money to purchase drugs rather than risk having them get involved with crime. "A lot of times they'd buy the stuff for me so I wouldn't get busted," an addict recalled. "They knew I was going to get it regardless, so they'd rather just give me the money" (Coombs & Coombs, 1988, p. 90). Although such teens may have been ignored as children, they now have the full focus of their family's attention.

Maintenance users vary in how easily they can extricate themselves from their addictions. Those who suffered emotional damage during childhood from negligent or abusive parents find it extremely difficult to stop using. That's because the chemicals temporarily cover up their deep emotional pain—their "psychache"—and help them cope with everyday life. These addicts do not recover without extensive help from others; they are psychologically as well as physically dependent on drugs.

Drug users who are only physically addicted—whose bodies, not minds, are dependent on chemicals—can usually quit once they realize that the problems of addiction outweigh the benefits. After suffering through the physical discomforts of detoxification, many choose to resume conventional activities.

Discontinuation and Relapse

Drug use may terminate abruptly with a fatal drug overdose—"a guy I knew wound up overdosing on drugs and they found him dead in a car"—or may be temporarily stopped if a teen is forced into participating in a treatment program. Drug users at the maintenance stage rarely quit voluntarily; they have burned bridges with the "straight" world and are committed to a lifestyle in which drugs take priority over everything else. The problem is that addicts don't see themselves as "losers" just because they use drugs. Many consider their lifestyle a kind of career, one in which they can move up the "ladder" and succeed or, if they lack resources and contacts, fail.

If you are successful, why change? Why change careers when you have invested so much time and energy getting there? You are absolutely wasting your time talking to someone about quitting when he has devoted a lot of his life to it and things are still going good for him. You have to catch him at a time when he has hit bottom and is discouraged (Coombs & Coombs, 1988, p. 91).

As we saw earlier, when drugs eventually stop producing highs, users take them just to feel normal. "At the end stage of my addiction," one user recalled, "I tried to mix this with that just to feel average. It wasn't to feel good—that was long gone." Emotional problems intensify. "I was suicidal and felt like I had just lost everything," one addict remembered. "I felt desperately evil and was beset with delusional, negative thoughts about everyone being out to get me. I was *totally* desperate."

In order for addicts to quit, life must become so bad for them that they see no other choice. "I'd been backed into a corner and was crying and sobbing when I realized that I had to go to any length to change things around," one said. "My life had become so unmanageable."

After so much goes wrong, the need for reform is obvious. But how does one do it? "I knew I had to change," one concluded, "but I didn't have an inkling as to what form that change should take." Rehabilitation centers may provide some hope. Unfortunately, however, "failed" addicts may use rehabilitation as a means of getting back on their feet in the drug world. They do this in the same way that people who file for bankruptcy to deal with financial failure may get a fresh start only to make the same kinds of choices again.

Like friends and family, detoxification centers sometimes play a utilitarian role for "burned-out" users. Because these centers provide a place to rest, to eat regularly, and to stop spending money on drugs, they can become "revolving doors." By various manipulations, many users enter and reenter them, returning each time to their substance use with renewed health and hope for success in their drug "career."

Incarceration may also force addicts to temporarily stop using drugs—providing, of course, that a prison controls drug trafficking. Prisons can unintentionally *reinforce* the drug lifestyle by providing opportunities for less experienced users to make new connections and "learn a little bit more." Incarceration also increases the social distance between users and "straight" society, for it defines users as criminals and law-enforcement officials ("the Man") as their persecutors. "When you are in jail," one young user said, "you realize that the enemy has got you" (Coombs & Coombs, 1988, p. 93).

For maintenance users, drug discontinuation and renewal can become an ongoing cycle. During these off-and-on-again periods, a user's family members' attitudes fluctuate. Initially, parents have high hopes for their teen's recovery, but by the second or third treatment attempt, they are understandably less optimistic. Still, addicts can often easily manipulate their parents. "I know all I have to do is call my dad," said a female user. "He'll feel sorry for me and say, 'Okay, you've been away [in treatment] for a month, come on home.' But I know that when I get there, I'll start the whole bullshit all over again" (Coombs & Coombs, 1988, pp. 94–95).

Because of all the attention they get, addicts at this stage sometimes describe their relationships with their parents as improved. Now that they've captured the full focus of their parents' attention, they receive care and concern. "Before I was unhappy at home; I didn't feel that I could talk to my mother at all," a female addict explained. "Now I have a good relationship with her. She just didn't know how to express herself and neither did I." "My father and I were never really that close," another remembered.

> He just worked all the time and was never around. We never sat down and talked with each other. Well, now he's showing a lot of concern for me. He's helped me with money, and he's talked to me and given me a lot of understanding. He tells me lots of things to look at about myself, you know. I just say, "Yeah, yeah," letting it go in one ear and out the other (Coombs & Coombs, 1988, p. 95).

Recovery

When users truly embark on the voyage of recovery, they face a whole new set of challenges. Recovering addicts must begin their emotional development at the place where they first started relying on drugs to cope with unpleasant feelings. Their emotional coping skills never developed—or have atrophied through lack of use. Now they must learn healthier ways to face life's ups and downs.

Sidebar 6.4: Recovering From Addiction

"In my recovery I've learned how to deal with stress. I've learned how to identify my feelings. Before, I never spoke out about how I felt. I never spoke to my family because I didn't want my parents hurt. I remember thinking, 'Oh no, this is hurting them.' Somehow I got that message and it was a terrible burden to carry as a kid. Now that I'm clean, I've learned to talk about my feelings and to gradually work them out through daily life experiences."

Recovering addicts usually abandon old drug-using friends and form new relationships, sometimes with people they've met in recovery centers. "At first I tried to hang onto my old friends, but since I didn't want to drink with them, I left them behind," one recovering alcoholic said. "Instead I've developed a whole new circle of friends."

Emotional development can proceed rapidly when recovering addicts engage in self-help programs. "I didn't have a lot of confidence in myself growing up and I felt insecure and inadequate most of the time," said a former user. "I used to accept responsibility for everyone. But now I know I'm only responsible for myself, and I can't fix other people nor should I try. I've learned to love myself."

A chemical-free lifestyle also goes a long way toward improving family relationships. "I'm finding as I get into a sober lifestyle that my relationships are many times better than before. The whole foundation of that is in not drinking."

Although all this may sound like a happy ending, any recovering user will counsel teens to avoid the allure of addiction's "golden handcuffs" by not starting in the first place. Like all bad habits, the early rewards are not worth the price required later on. Addicts can never replace lost years and lost opportunities, and recovery is not easy. "The toughest mountain I have ever climbed," an addict warned, "was in recovery."

A C T I V I T I E S   F O R   P A R E N T S   A N D   K I D S

6.1 Ask your kids what they think of media portrayals of people who are "under the influence." Is using drugs portrayed as "cool"? Funny? Pitiful? Why are users portrayed this way?

6.2 A young person tried to help an addicted friend and instead developed his own drug problem. How can teens help others escape addiction without getting sucked into the problem? Discuss possibilities and revisit the question as you continue through this book.

R E F E R E N C E S

Coombs, Robert H. 1997. *Drug-Impaired Professionals.* Cambridge, MA: Harvard University Press.
Coombs, Robert H., & Carol Jean Coombs. 1996. "Drug Testing Attitudes of Mandatory Participants." *Journal of Substance Misuse,* 1, pp. 85–90.
Coombs, Robert H., & Kathryn Coombs. 1988. "Developmental Stages in Drug Use: Changing Family Involvements." In *The Family Context of Adolescent Drug Use,* Ed. Robert H. Coombs. New York: The Haworth Press, pp. 73–98.

PART FOUR

Which Industries Promote Drug Use?

Imagine yourself in a wrestling ring with little or no formal training. You're about to compete simultaneously against several powerful, well-financed, and well-trained Sumo-like wrestlers. Although this scenario may seem a bit far-fetched, parents who try to keep their kids from drug entanglements are facing a similar challenge: They're competing against powerful industries that directly or indirectly profit from young people's drug use. Each industry spends billions of dollars annually to make psychoactive drugs (especially alcohol and tobacco) available and glamorous. Thus parents confront a formidable hurdle.

Let's size up these opponents.

CHAPTER

7 Drug-Producing Industries

Four giant industries produce most of the psychoactive chemicals we take into our bodies: the pharmaceutical industry, the tobacco industry, the alcoholic beverage industry, and the illicit-drug industry.

The Pharmaceutical Industry

An estimated one hundred thousand people in the United States die each year from prescription drugs (Abate & Howe, 2000). More than 2.4 billion prescriptions are reportedly written in the United States each year. Pharmaceutical companies spend about $20 billion annually developing pills and potions to cure everything from wrinkles and baldness and to prevent depression and stress. The payoff is awesome: A $300-billion-a-year pharmaceutical industry has become the most profitable industry in the Fortune 500 (Greenwald, 1998).

Producing more than four hundred thousand different drugs, the pharmaceutical industry has convinced the public that human suffering is a medical condition—and that drugs are the cure. People no longer accept pain and anguish as natural aspects of living.

Accustomed to "miracle drugs," most people uncritically accept drug therapy as inherently beneficial. "Much of our population," a pharmacist observed, "is conditioned to think that the first moment of mental, physical, or emotional discomfort is a signal for instant pharmaceutical treatment." The phrase "medicalization of the human condition" describes this mentality (Bernstein & Lennard, 1973, p. 23).

The pharmaceutical industry profits by exploiting this "feel-better-fast" attitude. "I haven't got time for the pain," say the lyrics from a popular song used in a television ad for a pain reliever.

Each year, this industry also spends more than $5 billion on marketing drugs to physicians—those gatekeepers of the legal drug industry. That's several thousand dollars for *every* doctor in the United States! Physicians receive numerous mailings, frequent visits from drug-company representatives bearing free samples, and occasionally trips to resorts where drug companies educate them about new drugs. One critic called these trips "the frequent prescriber travel plan" (Whitaker, 1991, p. 48).

Why are the drug companies' wooing doctors? Drug therapy makes many physicians' jobs quick and easy. "It's so much easier to write a prescription than to sit down and talk with the patient about his problem," one doctor admitted. "It's easy to normalize drug taking as part of the human condition" (Coombs, 1996, p. 190).

Even children get caught up in the drug-prescribing frenzy. In 1997, for example, more than eight hundred thousand North American children were given antidepressants by their parents and doctors (Kluger, 1998). One college student who had a job as a summer-camp counselor was astounded by the number of children on drugs for hyperactivity and depression. As one of his duties, he brought children to the nurse's office for their medications. "Many of these kids' parents were sedating their children so as to not be bothered by their typical rambunctious child behaviors."

Consider this tragic story. "Sally," a woman now in her forties, became addicted to amphetamines ("uppers") at age fourteen, when her pediatrician prescribed diet pills. "I weighed a hundred and nineteen pounds, and he said that according to his height chart I should weigh between a hundred and a hundred and five," she recalled.

> So, he prescribed diet pills and told me to stop eating cookies, donuts, pizza, malts—all the things I liked. I lost my appetite, didn't have to sleep, and was filled with energy all the time. It was great! I liked taking them, so I called his nurse and she gave me other prescriptions.

At the time, Sally, a straight-A student, was also student-body secretary, a cheerleader, and a tap dancer. Once she became addicted, however, her lifestyle spiraled downward to nightmarish depths. "I couldn't think in school anymore, I couldn't read, and I had to drop algebra and Spanish. In the ninth grade I went from straight A's to barely passing."

Because she wanted to lose even more weight, she kept dieting. "I kept taking the pills because I wanted to be super-skinny and wear a very small sized dress," she explained. When she became dehydrated, her doctor was alarmed. "He put me in the hospital and said that if I didn't eat they would feed me intravenously. When they tried to hold me down, I kicked them and knocked over the IV machine." Things got even worse.

> They transferred me to a psychiatric ward and started giving me librium and tranquilizers. I was in there for months—mostly sleeping. When I was awake I smoked lots of cigarettes; my Mom brought me a cartoon each week. After that I was defined as crazy and out of control—so I spent much of my teenage and young-adult years in hospitals, sedated on Thorazine. I've only recently gotten off these drugs and with a therapist's help started feeling like my real self again. I'm learning to think on my own, feel, and have energy.

In addition to prescription drugs, a variety of over-the-counter (non-prescription drugs) fill store shelves. For these substances, the U.S. Food and Drug Administration does not require manufacturers to report adverse effects, as it does for prescription drugs.

It's probably no coincidence that the upswing in worldwide drug use follows a period of intensive advertising by pharmaceutical companies. These ads have convinced the public that a chemical cure exists for every conceivable ailment, as well as every uncomfortable feeling. Drug use is now an acceptable, widespread aspect of everyday living. The belief in "better living through chemistry," a well-known commercial slogan, has become institutionalized in much of the industrialized world—to the ultimate detriment of our children.

The Tobacco Industry

Picture three fully loaded 747 jumbo jets crashing, killing everyone on board. Then imagine that tragedy happening every day. That's the toll that smoking exacts in this country—a mind-boggling 434,000 premature deaths every year from smoking-related diseases such as heart disease and lung cancer (Wellness Letter, 1993, p. 7).

Tobacco, a drug that is both addictive and lethal, is the leading cause of preventable death and disease in the developed world. It accounts for close to 20 percent of all fatalities. Cigarettes kill more people in the United States each year than the combined effects of alcohol, heroin, cocaine, and all other illicit drugs—plus all auto crashes, homicides, and suicides (www.infact.org/about.html).

If current smoking patterns continue, nearly one-tenth of the world's population will eventually be wiped out by tobacco-related diseases. This includes more than two hundred million of today's children and teenagers, two-thirds of whom reside in Third World countries (www.infact.org/about.html).

Researchers have conducted more than fifty thousand studies on the devastating effects of tobacco on health in dozens of countries. Worldwide, tobacco use causes about 90 percent of lung-cancer deaths, 30 percent of all cancers, 20–25 percent of coronary heart diseases and stroke deaths, and more than 80 percent of chronic bronchitis and emphysema (www.infact.org/about.html).

Sidebar 7.1: Tobacco Companies Respond to "Customer Deaths"

You discover your product kills one-third of your customers. In response, you:

A. Launch a massive product recall
B. Introduce a "safer" product that isn't
C. Argue in court that the research isn't conclusive
D. Run some ads about how you give to charity

Did you choose "A"? The tobacco companies didn't. In response to customer deaths, one company launched a "safer" cigarette that's actually as deadly as ever. Another company claimed in court that there wasn't scientific proof that smoking caused cancer. That same company is now using PR [public relations] to smooth things over, spending $100 million to advertise $60 million in charity. The tobacco companies say they're changing. Their choices tell a different story. [For more information, visit this website (www.americanlegacy.org) or see *The New York Times* article by Stuart Elliott, "Tired of Being a Villain, Philip Morris Works on Its Image," November 11, 1999] (American Legacy Foundation, 2001, p. B14).

The tobacco industry uses an effective strategy of disputing evidence of tobacco's health effects, building a lobby powerful enough to defy public opinion in U.S. lawmaking, and enlisting the support of the government in imposing its deadly product and practices on other countries (www.infact.org/about.html).

Despite the addictive nature of tobacco, the tobacco industry targets children and young people, preying on those who rarely understand addiction's perils. A survey of U.S. high school daily smokers found that although only 5 percent of those teenagers thought that they would "definitely" be smoking five years later, nearly 75 percent of them still smoked every day seven to nine years later (www.infact.org/about.html).

Sidebar 7.2: Tobacco Buys Influence in Congress

- Currently, there are 209 tobacco company lobbyists on Capitol Hill, one for every 2.5 members of Congress
- Members of Congress who finance their political campaigns with tobacco money vote with cigarette makers 9-15 times more often those who do not
- Tobacco companies put more than $25 million in campaign coffers. "They are clearly the most powerful lobby in the country, period," said Paul Billings of the American Lung Association. "But

they have a huge problem despite all the money they spend. Their product kills people!" (David Phinney, "Tobacco Cash Buys Influence," ABCNEWS.com, May 6, 1999.)

A 1998 survey of more than sixteen thousand U.S. students conducted by the Centers for Disease Control and Prevention (CDC) revealed that 70 percent had tried cigarettes at least once. (The percentage is probably even higher among teenagers overall, because the survey did not include dropouts (Associated Press, 1998). Between 33 percent and 50 percent of people who experiment with cigarettes become regular smokers. But now researchers have found that smokers develop a pattern of nicotine addiction and a desire to quit in their teenage years. "They start to smoke because they want an image, they want to make a statement, they get seduced by the advertising," a CDC executive said. "But after a few years they realize it is costly, it is messy, it interferes with performance and it no longer gives them the cachet it gave them when they were twelve to thirteen years old" (Associated Press, 1998). Specifically, 9.2 percent of middle school and 28.4 percent of high school students said they are cigarette smokers. Unless these trends are reversed, said the CDC director, "five million children under the age of eighteen alive today in the United States will die prematurely as a result of cigarette addiction" (Cimons, 2000, p. A19).

The Alcoholic-Beverage Industry

The advertising industry deluges kids and young adults with promotional messages that portray drinking as an essential feature of social life, a way to enhance popularity and well-being. Though beer ads are directed mostly at young adults—the primary drinking age is twenty-one to twenty-nine— these messages affect teenagers as well.

If junior and senior high school students are the tobacco industry's most valuable recruits, college students are the alcoholic-beverage industry's primary target. Drinking is highly glamorized on college campuses, and sports events rely heavily on income from alcohol advertising. If the beer cans emptied by American college students were stacked end-to-end, the stack would reach seventy thousand miles beyond the moon (Eigen, 1991).

The alcoholic-beverage industry reportedly spends one billion dollars annually to advertise its products, and lobbies heavily for favorable public policy. It also utilizes the new electronic media to promote a favorable view of its industry and product. The Marin Institute for the Prevention of Alcohol and Other Drug Problems regularly analyzes this industry's messages. It notes that although the messages put a positive spin on alcohol—it's as "American as apple pie"—alcohol-related problems kill and impair hundreds of thousands (www.marininstitute.org/industry.html).

Sidebar 7.3: Beer-Company Cafeteria

"We used to serve beer in our cafeteria to employees on their lunch hours and rest breaks, but we don't anymore," said a beer-industry executive to a federal official. "Why did you stop?" the visitor asked. "Why do you think?" the executive responded (Livsey, 1993).

Common Cause, another watchdog group, reports that "Congress usually backs down to big booze." Wielding its money, contacts, and lobbying might, the alcohol industry has for years successfully defeated attempts to increase federal taxes on liquor. "And at the same time Congress is raising excise taxes on tobacco, it's actually considering a rollback of some taxes on alcoholic beverages" (www.commoncause.org/publications).

The U.S. government spends billions every year on the war on drugs, yet as U.S. congressman Joseph Kennedy noted, it lets the alcohol industry tell young people that if they "want to get a pretty girl or win a bike race, they ought to go suck a brew" (www.commoncause.org/publications/booze6.htm). Kennedy sponsored several proposals to control the alcohol advertising industry, including a bill that would have banned all broadcast advertising of hard-liquor products.

The alcohol lobby flexed its muscle in Washington while fighting a bill that proposed a tough national definition of drunk driving. After the bill's defeat in the House, Mothers Against Drunk Driving (MADD) spokeswoman Brandy Anderson accused Rules Committee members of "listening to the money. They did not act on the voice of America. Safety doesn't talk down here. Money talks" (www.commoncause.org/publications/booze6.htm).

The Illicit-Drug Industry

A few decades ago, drugs were generally unavailable to adolescents. Although alcohol was accessible, social pressure from close-knit communities discouraged its abuse.

Times have changed. Youth can now easily access alcohol, over-the-counter medications, *and* illicit drugs. And the use of these substances, modeled by cultural heroes, is not only acceptable, it is often glamorized. "It's no big deal getting drugs," a user boasted. "Piece of cake." "It's ridiculously easy," another said. When a psychologist asked a drug user where he got his drugs, he replied, "Any high school."

What explains this availability? The answer is supply and demand. Though adolescents are prohibited by law to buy alcoholic beverages, many find it easy to circumvent those laws. Often, neighborhood convenience stores only exacerbate the problem, selling beer to minors on demand. The illicit-drug trade is itself a hugely profitable, sophisticated industry. Major distributors use advanced technology to transport and distribute products. Even teenage street gangs now employ electronic surveillance devices to avoid detection. Currently, the demand for illegal drugs is so high and the profit margin so large that suppliers thrive despite the risk of severe penalties.

Sidebar 7.4: Cocaine Trade

In the past decade, the cocaine trade alone reportedly became a $30 billion industry; if ranked among Fortune 500 businesses, it would be listed seventh. The international retail of illicit drugs now exceeds that of the world's oil trade and is second only to worldwide arms sales (*Prevention Pipeline*, 1996, pp. 13, 15).

Prescription drugs—pain killers, stimulants, and tranquilizers—are among the most abused substances and are easily obtained illegally. About 2.6 million people in the United States use these drugs for nonmedical reasons—more than the estimated use of heroin, crack, and cocaine combined. It's a fairly simple process to go to a doctor, get a prescription, and have the pharmacy fill it and the insurance company pay for it. One California woman reportedly duped forty-two doctors and twenty-six pharmacies into giving her thousands of codeine tablets. Only marijuana use is more widespread (Jalon, 1986).

A few unscrupulous physicians, dentists, and pharmacists make enormous profits dispensing prescriptions dishonestly. They have turned their practices into lucrative pill-mills. The Drug Enforcement Agency estimates that several hundred million doses of prescription drugs are diverted each year to illicit use ("Prescription Drug Monitoring: States Can Readily Identify Illegal Sales and Use of Controlled Substances," 1992).

Other entrepreneurs profit from drug production and sales. With relatively little effort, an amateur chemist can develop and sell "designer drugs," slight variations on illegal substances such as heroin. A Canadian college student, for example, a two-time science fair winner during junior high school, became a millionaire by selling Ecstasy made in his underground laboratory. At age 19, two years into his computer science program, he attended his first rave. "I became pretty immersed in the rave culture," he acknowledged, and started making his own drugs. He bought specialized equipment at chemical supply stores, imported chemicals and used buckets and bowls. "I have always had an interest in the chemistry of drugs," he said, "so this was my way of making a contribution to the rave scene."

His peers provided an enthusiastic response. "The feedback is overwhelmingly positive from whatever group of friends you give the drugs to," he said, describing his early trafficking as a "social accommodation." "There was more than I needed and I was involved in a community." But the profit motive soon complemented his idealism. "It was hard," he said. "I was going to school during the day and doing raves at night. There was little room for anything else."

After police raided his lab and arrested him on various drug charges, he pleaded guilty on six of 17 drug offenses and was sentenced to two years in prison. "You are a very intelligent individual who is more than capable of making a very significant contribution," said the judge when sentencing him. "Instead, you got involved in the drug subculture. Intelligence is a two-edged sword" (Humphreys, 2000).

For less than $1,000, a reporter legally purchased all the ingredients necessary to produce a batch of methamphetamine with a street value of $40,000 to $60,000. In a two-month period, one young white collar worker reportedly supplemented his $40,000 annual income by $25,000 through cocaine dealing. Some middle-class suburbanites cultivate marijuana plants in their backyards to provide for their own needs and sell the rest for profits.

The government's "war on drugs" relies on law enforcement and the criminal-justice system to monitor and control today's drug problems. Yet, despite increased federal funding ($1.65 billion in 1982 to $17.7 billion in 1999), making more arrests, and hiring more agents, the drug war is losing ground (Office of National Drug Control Policy, 1992; 2000). Last year more than half of all graduating seniors tried an illegal drug and nearly 89 percent agreed that it was "fairly easy" or "very easy" to obtain marijuana (Johnston, Bachman, & O'Malley, 1999). A bigger, better, and more efficient government "war" is not making the desired impact.

Officials intercept only a small percentage of the narcotics smuggled into this country, and as their efforts to stem the flow intensify, the monetary value of the drugs coming in only escalates. One official said that trying to stop the flow of drugs is like trying to pump out water from a hole at the bottom of the ocean.

Despite recurring presidential declarations of war on drugs, the destructive use of legal and illegal drugs in America continues unabated. Currently one in 144 Americans resides in jail; most of these individuals were incarcerated for drug-related offenses. One in every twenty Americans born in 1997 will spend some time in jail (Califano, 1998).

Sidebar 7.5: Drug War

The so-called drug war began in the late 1960s involving only two federal agencies with a combined budget of less than $10 million. By 1993, the number of agencies had grown to 54, including every branch of the armed forces. In the year 2000 the overall budget has climbed to $19.2 billion. Yet, drug-related deaths are at record highs, drugs are more available, cheaper, and purer than ever before and most addicts needing treatment do not receive it (The Lindesmith Center, www.dpf.org/archive/2000).

Federal policies, based on a catch-'em-and-lock-'em-up approach, fail to grasp the importance of the American family in stemming the use of drugs. The U.S. government has allocated most of its budget to enforcement, swelling prison populations at great public expense, with little or no impact on the underlying problem or its impact on families.

ACTIVITIES FOR PARENTS AND KIDS

7.1 Discuss the billion-dollar industry behind kids' smoking. If you were a tobacco company executive, how would you market to your target audience (teens) while pretending not to? Examine ad campaigns. Check out the marketing of cigarettes in Third World countries. Teen smoking has gone up in the past decade—ask your kids why they think that's happened.

7.2 Discuss the billion-dollar industry behind kids' drinking. How much money do companies spend supporting college drinking (advertising, parties, give aways)? Are keg parties a "rebellious" fraternity tradition, or a corporate-sponsored opportunity to develop students' loyalty to a particular beer? College students are often perceived as brighter and more sophisticated than their peers who aren't in school. Yet, statistically speaking, college students drink a lot more than their noncollege counterparts. How would you and your kids explain that?

REFERENCES

Abate, Tom, & Kenneth Howe. 2000. "Debate Intensifies Over Safety of Herbal Remedies." *San Francisco Chronicle*, Monday, April 3, A1.

American Legacy Foundation (advertisement). 2001. *Los Angeles Times*, February 2, p. B14.

Associated Press. 1998. "Of Teens Who Try Cigarettes, 36% Gain a Habit, Survey Finds," May 22.

Bernstein, Arnold, & Lennard, H. L. 1973. "Drugs, Doctors & Junkies." *Society* 10 (May–June), pp. 14–25.

Califano, Joseph A. 2000. "The Government Should Direct Its Resources Toward Drug Treatment." *Addiction: Opposing Viewpoints*. San Diego: Greenhaven Press, pp. 160–163.

Cimons, Marlene. 2000. "9.2% in Middle School Are Smokers, Study Says." *Los Angeles Times*, January 28, p. A19.

Coombs, R. H. 1996. "Addicted Health Professionals." *Journal of Substance Misuse I*, pp. 187–194.

Eigen, L. 1991. *Alcohol Practices, Policies, and Potentials of American Colleges and Universities Center*. Washington, DC: Office for Substance Abuse Prevention (OSAP).

Greenwald, John. 1998. "Drug Quest: Magic Bullets for Boomers (Success of Viagra and Other Lifestyle-Enhancing Drugs)." *Time*, May 4, 54 (2 pps).

Humphreys, Adrian. 2000. "Student's Secret Lab Made Drugs Worth $1M." *National Post*, Thursday, June 1, p. A10.

Jalon, Allan. 1986. "Deep Inside the Pill Trade." *Los Angeles Times*, June 8, pp. 10–15; 23–26.

Johnston, L., Bachman, J., & O'Malley, P. 1999. *Monitoring the Future: National Results on Adolescent Drug Use Overview of Key Findings, 1999*. Washington, DC: NIDA, 2000, pp. 3–6.

Kluger, Jeffrey. 1998. "Next Time Up, Prozac." *Time*. November 30, p. 94.

Livsey, Laury. 1993. "The Beer Facts." *The New Era*, March, pp. 45–58.

Office of National Drug Control Policy. 1992. *National Drug Control Strategy: Budget Summary*. Washington DC: U.S. Government Printing Office.

Office of National Drug Control Policy. 2000. *National Drug Control Strategy: 2000 Annual Report*. Washington DC: U.S. Government Printing Office, p. 94.

Phinney, David. 1999. "Tobacco Cash Buys Influence." ABCNEWS.com, May 6.

"Prescription Drug Monitoring: States Can Readily Identify Illegal Sales and Use of Controlled Substances." 1992. Gaithersburg, MD: U.S. General Accounting Office.

Prevention Pipeline. 1996. March/April, pp. 13, 15.

Wellness Letter. 1993. U.C. Berkeley, 9(9), June, p. 7.

Whitaker, Eric. 1991. "Ethics of a Doughnut." *The New Physician*, September, p. 48.

INTERNET SOURCES

www.commoncause.org/publications/booze6.htm
www.infact.org/about.html
www.marininstitute.org/industry.html
The Lindesmith Center at www.dpf.org/archive/2000

CHAPTER

8 Drug-Glamorizing Industries

Six other industries besides tobacco, alcohol, pharmaceuticals, and illegal drugs play a large role in addiction—the entertainment, media, music, fashion, paraphernalia, and advertising industries. All of these glamorize the drug lifestyle, making it appeal that much more to young people.

Indeed, the street jargon used by addicts and dealers gets popularized by the media, and thus finds its way into the speech of the TV-watching public.

> "The influence of the media should not be underestimated," noted Barry R. McCaffrey, former Director of the Office of National Drug Control Policy. "By mid-adolescence, kids have watched about 15,000 hours of television—more time than they spend with teachers in school. Add to that figure the hours devoted to video games, watching tapes on the VCR, listening to the radio and attending movies, and the media's impact becomes primary" (McCaffrey, 1997, p. B7).

The Media and Music Industries

The advent of television in U.S. households in the late 1940s dramatically altered the recreational habits of families. Perhaps "the good old days" weren't as rosy as we sometimes imagine, but the truth remains that TV quickly elbowed out many a family bike ride or game of catch.

Now television not only dominates leisure and family time, it powerfully affects our attitudes, behaviors, and relationships. Like any other kind of communication, TV teaches viewers through what it portrays. More specifically, kids often look to television for role models.

The occasional antidrug program delivered at school can hardly compete with what appears to kids as the "reality" portrayed on television. Keep in mind that TV programs and ads are produced by talented writers, artists, musicians, and marketing experts. For commercial reasons, then, the goal of any TV programming is to attract and stimulate viewers. In many cases, this means high-action episodes that glamorize alcohol, crime, and street life. An ongoing mental diet of such messages during childhood no doubt takes its toll.

The film industry is another powerful prodrug voice. To say that movies changed during the past decade is an understatement; what was once considered shocking is now accepted and commonplace. "Movies bear more resemblance to tobacco advertising than they do to reality," says Dr. Stanton Glantz, a professor of medicine at the University of California, San Francisco. Glantz had analyzed the portrayal of smoking in movies. "Kids come away thinking that the habit is widely accepted, practiced by people in positions of power, when it's actually minority behavior concentrated among the less-educated and the poor." Glantz points out that smoking among lead actors in top-grossing films is four times the rate of smoking in the general population (Dutka, 1996, p. F10).

A 1996 study found that 77 percent of 133 current movies portrayed smoking as rebellious and "cool." Tobacco companies paid one movie company $350,000 to show their product in the 1989 hit movie *License to Kill*. Although studios reportedly began to refuse such funds, Glantz points out that "... money is changing hands at some level. Water doesn't run uphill" (Dutka, 1996, p. F11).

One powerful trend, all the more striking because it goes unchallenged, is the inclusion of festive, unsupervised teen-drinking scenes in most films featuring high school students. In fact, it is difficult to find a movie about high school (or college) kids that does not feature such a scene. Because these movies are usually rated PG-13, their audience easily includes middle school students and even young children. Over and over, the message boldly exclaims that illegal, underage drinking is normal and fun.

As in television, some films glamorize criminal life as well as the use of alcohol, tobacco, and other drugs. Unfortunately, some movie directors use drinks and cigarettes as props, giving actors something to do with their hands while they talk. The cumulative effect shapes our entire culture, especially the attitudes and behaviors of our children.

In 1999, the White House released a study examining the two hundred most popular movie rentals and one thousand of the most popular songs from 1996 and 1997. Findings revealed that

- 98 percent of movies and 28 percent of songs depict illicit drugs, alcohol, or tobacco;
- illicit drugs appeared in 22 percent of movies;
- fewer than 15 percent of young characters who smoked marijuana or cigarettes experienced any apparent consequences;
- 26 percent of movies portrayed illicit drug use in a humorous context;
- illicit drug use was associated with wealth or luxury in 20 percent of the songs in which drugs appeared; sexual activity in 30 percent; crime or violence in 20 percent;
- although there are few African-American characters in movies, these characters were portrayed as using drugs at a disproportionately high rate;

- alcohol and tobacco were used in over 76 percent of movies rated G or PG and in an overwhelming majority of PG-13 movies (tobacco 82 percent; alcohol 94 percent)

(www.samhsa.gov/press/99/990428nr.html).

The same White House study shows that 63 percent of rap songs refer to illicit drugs and 27 percent of all songs relate to drugs and alcohol (Lichtblau, 1999). When the president of the National Academy of Recording Arts and Sciences proposed anonymous confidential reporting of drug-using members, he met intense opposition from high-level record executives. Speaking anonymously, one label executive questioned, "Why doesn't he stop butting in on record company business where he doesn't belong and go back to things he knows, like giving out Grammys?" (Hochman, 1996, p. F1).

The music industry, strongly associated with drug use and prodrug messages, periodically suffers bad publicity from the overdosing deaths of famous artists. In the mid-1990s, at least four well-known rock musicians died of drug-related causes within a two-year period. Ironically, even these deaths may make drugs seem exciting to risk-seeking teens. When Jonathan Melvoin—a musician for the Smashing Pumpkins, one of the country's most successful alternative-rock bands—overdosed on "Red Rum" ("murder" spelled backwards), his death spawned a macabre surge in sales of this brand of heroin (Goldman, 1996).

The Fashion Industry

The fashion industry also promotes and glamorizes drug use. Although fashion-industry executives don't want to discuss it, stories circulate about well-known models and their "smack" (heroin) habits. A July 1996 expose in *Allure* magazine, for example, highlighted the career of one model and her $200-a-day heroin habit. "The 90's," noted fashion reporter Amy Spindler to *The New York Times* in 1993, ". . . may well be remembered as the decade when fashion served as a pusher—of what appears to be the best-dressed heroin addicts in history." (Konigsberg, 1996, p. 92). Yet, when some of the top fashion industry executives were asked about this, typical denial responses ran the gamut of, "If it's happening, it's not my girls," to "I don't know if they're doing it, and I'd rather not" (Konigsberg, 1996, p. 92).

Sidebar 8.1: Heroin Chic

At least since the 1960s, fashionable models have aimed to be thin, sometimes with such determination that they have become anorexic or have suffered other medical problems. In the mid-1990s, this waif-like image was accentuated even more. Models looked "hung over," with dark circles under glazed eyes. This look, which some people in the fashion business thought was attractive to young people, was portrayed in a notorious set of advertisements for Calvin Klein clothes in 1997. It was dubbed "heroin chic" because the models looked like drug addicts. In fact, there are well-substantiated reports that heroin addiction is common among fashion photographers and models, so the look is not necessarily always simulated (from Michael B. Quinion, 1997, in www.clever. net/quinion/words/turnsofphrase/tp-her1.htm).

Heroin replaced cocaine a few years ago as the "chic" drug among younger celebrities, rock stars, and models. "The modeling business is a real snob system, like high school," a modeling executive explained.

> You are either in the sorority or not. There is a group of girls in the top echelon who do the top shows, who sort of bandy about and keep the other girls out. When the big girls go out back at the shows with their heroin, it's very freakish and the other girls want to be part of the team (Konigsberg, 1996, p. 92).

For a time, "heroin chic" insinuated itself into U.S. homes through fashion photography. These images redefined glamour as languor and helplessness. The standard of beauty became a pale complexion and a "waif" look, with bloodshot eyes and disheveled hair. Most parents were probably unaware that during the "Kate Moss" fashion era, the current style was meant to portray heroin addiction. Ironically, many models didn't find it too hard to capture that look. One was shocked when she thumbed through a British fashion magazine featuring a young woman with half-open black eyes in an ill-fitting, skimpy cocktail dress, her head tilted back in drugged oblivion. She realized that the women in the picture was her, but she didn't remember the pictures being taken.

Sidebar 8.2: A U.S. President's Concern

U.S. president Bill Clinton accused the fashion industry of glamorizing drugs with trendy "heroin-chic" photographs of gaunt, glazed-eyed models. In his address to U.S. mayors, Clinton said that heroin use was on the rise, and cited the fashion images as a major reason. "You need not glamorize addiction to sell clothes," said Clinton. "Our society cannot say, on one hand, we want to have a tough, intolerant attitude toward drugs and, on the other hand, send a very different message every time there might be a little money made out of it."

Clinton's comments came after an article appeared in *The New York Times* about the heroin-chic style, made popular through the work of photographer David Sorrenti. Sorrenti, twenty, endured some criticism about his style of photography, and died a heroin-related death in February. Magazines began calling for an end to this "strung-out," haunted, look. "We now see in college campuses and neighborhoods [that] heroin is becoming increasingly the drug of choice. And we know that part of this has to do with the images that are finding their way to our young people" (*The Ottawa Citizen*, May 22, 1997, cited in www.media-awareness.ca/eng/news/news/drugs.htm).

These incidents may seem far removed from your children's lives—until you see teens scouring fashion magazines for guidance on how to look and act. Teens don't just get crushes on celebrities, they try to be as much like them as possible. Thanks to the pervasiveness of music, film, television, and the print media, kids get exposed to these influences early in life. As one seven-year-old girl recently wrote in her school journal, "I love Britney Spears [teen pop star] because she is so pretty. I wish she could be my Mother."

The Drug-Paraphernalia Industry

Paraphernalia—items used to prepare, package, store, and use illegal drugs—became available in the mid-1960s when marijuana smokers gravitated toward novelty shops for such items as rolling papers, bongs (a water pipe for cooling smoke so the user can inhale more), roach-clips (used to hold the cigarette), and pipes. These "counterculture" items soon became popular. Because demand for them greatly exceeded supply, a high mark-up of these items guaranteed big profits.

Drug paraphernalia, the ultimate glamorization of drug use, have been openly sold and advertised. These objects communicate an image of drugs as acceptable, even respectable and commonplace. Adolescents who visit "head shops" are intrigued by the fancy tools and accessories. Kids still attracted by toys and games of dress-up can buy drug-related trinkets and related clothing, decorative items, and permanent or temporary tattoos. One teen, for example, wore tiny, silver "cocaine-spoon" earrings to school.

This industry's growth has been explosive. In the early 1970s, paraphernalia for marijuana smokers were manufactured and widely advertised. Since 1974, three trade publications and ten consumer-oriented magazines devoted to the topic have emerged.

Although some states have enacted antiparaphernalia laws, few cities devote any significant effort to enforcing them. Raids on retail stores often get dismissed in court. Defense attorneys argue that the laws are too vague, and that they require store owners to use clairvoyance to identify customer intent.

The paraphernalia industry boomed in the mid-1990s. Despite laws against selling and transporting such items, enterprising young capitalists produced thousands of pipes and bongs. One entrepreneur and his assistant, turning out a hundred hand-crafted bongs each week, sold their wares to two dozen shops in the Los Angeles area. Bongs may cost about $20 to make, but some may sell for as much as $170. One manufacturer claimed three hundred out-of-state wholesale customers.

The paraphernalia industry aggressively expanded its market by reinvesting profits in high-technology product research and development, working to create a more visible and acceptable image for its wares. A massive mail-order component now generates substantial profits. One company grosses $600,000 annually and advertises on cable television, attracting about 60 percent of its customers this way. Some stores also sell legitimate items such as clothing, foreign cigarettes, and cigars. One head shop that features an art gallery and a juice bar entertains customers with glass blowers. "Can't we all get a bong together?" another shop advertises.

Paraphernalia businessmen skirt the law by posting signs in their stores reading that bongs and other pipes are intended only for the use of tobacco and that they are not sold to anyone under age eighteen. Signs also warn customers that those who mention "crack pipes," "shaker vials," or "bongs" will be refused service. "Customers must sign statements declaring they will not use purchases with illegal drugs," reads another sign. Thanks to such caveats, these items are more widely available than ever. Teens can shop for them while they're out looking for clothes, jewelry, and video games (Gellene, 1996).

The Advertising Industry

Media messages saturate an adolescent's environment, touting the benefits of alcohol, tobacco, and prescription and over-the-counter drugs.

Although cigarette ads have been banned from TV and radio since 1971, tobacco companies sponsor sporting events shown on TV and plaster their names anywhere they can. During one ninety-minute car race, for example, the word "Marlboro" appeared on TV 5,933 times! (www.cdc.gov/tobacco/sgr-4kids/adbust.html).

Sidebar 8.3: Tobacco Marketing

To find new customers, U.S. tobacco companies spend $11 million every day to advertise and promote cigarettes—more than the U.S. Federal Office on Smoking and Health has spent to prevent smoking in an entire year (www.infact.org/youth.html).

Even without TV commercials, the tobacco industry spends about $5 billion a year on advertising, more than any other except the auto industry. It's no surprise that the top three brands of cigarettes that underage smokers use are the three that spend the most on advertising: Marlboro, Camel, and Newport. And these ads reach children as well. Studies show that children are just as familiar with "Joe Camel" as they are with Mickey Mouse. Three- and six-year-old children—30 percent and 60 percent, respectively—match "Joe Camel" with a cigarette. "It doesn't take a Ph.D. to tell you that cartoon characters on skateboards are not targeting middle-aged professional women," one critic noted (www.bu.edu/cohis/smoking/upsmoke/whysmoke.htm).

Worse, the U.S. public helps finance such ads. The U.S. Congress lets the $60-billion tobacco industry deduct the cost of cigarette ads from their taxes—a subsidy financed through higher taxes on average U.S. citizens.

As public outcry and lawsuits make marketing in the United States more difficult for the tobacco industry, the vulnerable, unrestricted Third World market becomes a greater target. "Many African children have two hopes," noted Kenyan physician Paul Wangai. "One is to go to heaven, the other to America" (www.infact.org/youth.html). U.S. tobacco companies capitalize on these desires by advertising messages that associate smoking with affluence. It's not uncommon to hear children say that they take up smoking because of the glamorous lifestyle associated with it. Notice that the tobacco industry specifically targets the uneducated and naive: children who lack judgment, people who lack economic opportunities, those who lack information. At rock concerts and discos in eastern Europe, for example, young women in cowgirl outfits give away free Philip Morris Marlboro's. Teenagers who accept a "light" on the spot receive a pair of Marlboro sunglasses.

Alcohol is so successfully marketed that many people regard it as an integral part of successful living. Advertisers persuade us that alcoholic beverages will enhance our lives. Moreover, the ads suggest that if someone gets into trouble because of drinking, it's his or her personal responsibility— it has nothing to do with the way the product is manufactured, marketed, or sold. Advertisers also link this commonly used drug with success in relationships—at school, work, and play. The message? Whatever we do, we can do it better with a drink.

Sidebar 8.4: Advertising to Children

The amount of time children spend watching television (25 hours a week on the average) and listening to radio, combined with the alcohol industry's high advertising budget on product marketing to the broadcast media ($682.6 million in 1995) shape youth attitude about drinking (www.samhsa.gov/oop/qfullhit). Not only is drinking portrayed in fun-filled commercials (as many as 5000 beer and wine commercials each year and at least 2500 liquor ads in major magazines), but it is also regularly glamorized during prime-time and other programming. A child will see alcohol consumed on television thousands of times before reaching the legal drinking age of 21.

Brewers and distillers reportedly spent $1.9 billion in a recent year to support entertainment programs aimed primarily at young people. One brewing company, for example, sponsored three thousand rock concerts, of which six hundred were either on or adjacent to a college campus. U.S. college students spend about one-third of their discretionary income—$2–3 billion a year—on purchasing alcohol. About one-third of the revenue for college newspapers comes from beer and other alcohol advertisers. And alcohol-related traffic accidents continue to be the leading cause of death for young people in the United States (www.marininstitute.org/industry.html).

Commercials—especially those that use cartoons, sports themes, or attractive models—rivet kids' attention and promote the message that alcohol and tobacco enhance popularity, friendship, adventure, achievement, masculinity, sex appeal, and true love. Studies show that children retain the information in these ads and develop favorable beliefs about drinking. Fifth- and sixth-grade children who view these ads tend to agree with the statement, "Having a few beers is a good reward."

Alcoholic-beverage advertisers give children the impression that drinking alcohol is wonderful, then they add the postscript that kids must wait until they're twenty-one to drink. But of course teens don't wait. Why postpone all this popularity, conviviality, adventure, excitement, and sex appeal when they can have it now?

Although every ounce of alcohol sold adds about one dollar to the national cost of violence, advertising agencies continue to market alcoholic beverages as if they were as wholesome as vegetable soup. Fortunately, some advertising executives apparently do have a conscience. In 1985 the Partnership for a Drug-Free America, a volunteer organization, persuaded 250 big-name ad agencies from Los Angeles, New York City, Chicago, and other cities to volunteer their time and talent to create new and better ways to deglamorize drugs. Within a decade—thanks to the Partnership's high-powered connections—television networks, newspapers, magazines, and other media outlets donated more than $2 billion in free space and time toward this mission. A group of top executives from leading ad agencies now meet regularly to ensure that their best and brightest writers and producers create ads that inform youngsters about the consequences of using drugs. One marketing executive got involved when his seven-year-old son was offered marijuana on a school playground. "I figured if it can happen in

Greenwich [Connecticut] it can happen anywhere," he said. "No kid is safe. Not yours, not mine" (Warrick, 1996, p. E8). Ironically, these ad agencies also sell billions of dollars in alcohol advertisements.

Can the damage caused by such highly influential, prodrug industries be reversed? Can attitudes change in an entire generation that has matured in an environment saturated with prodrug messages? What can parents do?

ACTIVITIES FOR PARENTS AND KIDS

8.1 Keep a notebook by the TV. For one week, each time you notice a drug portrayed or mentioned on TV—including cigarettes, alcohol, and prescription drugs—note it. Then, score the incident as positive, negative, or neutral. For example, "Hero drinks beer with his best friend—positive." (You may want to give points and a prize for the family member who finds the most examples.) At the end of the week, discuss your findings as a family. Apart from antidrug ads, does any media appearance or mention of these substances suggest anything negative or neutral about that product?

8.2 Become savvy consumers of advertising. Use the list of fallacies, or deceptive "logic," that advertisers often employ, along with examples you'll find in Appendix B. Have a contest with your kids: Who can find an example of each fallacy first in TV, radio, and print ads during the coming week or two? The winner gets a prize, of course!

8.3 Become a member of the Parents Television Council and receive their monthly Newsletter, *PTC Insider.* This nondenominational organization of concerned parents, a volunteer media watchdog group, exerts pressure directly on advertisers of offensive programs that glamorize foul material like adultery, lewdness, raunch, and violence. PTC also enlists other organizations to do the same. Recently, for example, the American Academy of Pediatrics, the American Psychological Association, the American Academy of Child and Adolescent Psychiatry, and the American Medical Association jointly signed a PTC letter that voiced their concern over violent content in the media and emphasized the causal connection between such content and aggressive behavior in children. Contact PTC at P.O. Box 7802, Burbank, CA 91510-9817 and on the Internet (www.ParentsTV.org). Receive their twice-weekly e-mail report about industry news, show content, and *PTC* initiatives by sending your name and e-mail address to kcurtis@parentstv.org.

REFERENCES

Dutka, Elaine. 1996. "Force of Habit." *Los Angeles Times*, September 5, pp. F1, F10–F11.

Gellene, Denise. 1996. "A Boom in the Bong Business." *Los Angeles Times*. December 5, p. A1.

Goldman, John J. 1996. "Musician's Death Spurs Heroin Demand." *Los Angeles Times*, July 16, p. A5.

Hochman, Steve. 1996. "Flip Side to Pop Music's Drug War." *Los Angeles Times*, August 5,
    p. F1.
Konigsberg, Eric. 1996. "A Model Addiction." *Allure*, July, pp. 90–95.
Lichtblau, Eric. 1999. "Frequency of Drugs in Films, Music Studies." *Los Angeles Times*, April
    29, p. A4.
McCaffrey, Barry. 1997. "Mass manipulation of young minds." *Los Angeles Times*, *116(2)*,
    January 2, p. B7.
Quinion, Michael B. 1997 cited in www.clever,net/quinion/words/turnsofphrase/tp-herl.
    htm
Warrick, Pamela. 1996. "Can You Just Say No?" *Los Angeles Times*, August 30, pp. E1, E8.

INTERNET   SOURCES

www.cdc.gov/tobacco/
www.marininstitute.org/industry.html
www.bu.edu/cohis/smoking/upsmoke/whysmoke.html
www.samhsa.gov
www.media-awareness.caleng/news/news/drugs.htm
www.infact.org/youth.html

PART FIVE

What Can I Do at Home?

Okay, so now that you understand your youngster's vulnerabilities, the developmental stages of drug use, and your common foes, what can you do?

Remember, prevention is much easier than cure. Because drugs and alcohol give the illusion of meeting your youngsters' very real needs, your goals as a parent must be, first, to meet some of those needs yourself and, second, to help your growing children learn to meet their own needs in ways that enhance rather than diminish their health and happiness. These efforts will strengthen your overall family life.

Even if a family member is already struggling with an addiction, these techniques can make a difference.

CHAPTER

9 Build Friendships by Giving Love Supplies

The most important thing you can do to prevent drug abuse is to increase your influence by building friendships with your children. Give "love supplies," as psychologist Sterling Ellsworth calls activities that energize relationships. Spend time with them, smile, praise, touch, and listen. "It's important that parents be part of their kids' lives," a parent educator and community worker emphasized. "Build a friendship with them so that when they hit fifteen or sixteen and want to be independent, you will still have some influence. Everything we do in those first twelve years should build healthy relationships based on trust and good will."

Family Closeness

Youths who abstain from drugs typically have warm feelings toward their parents. In a study of 225 adolescent drug users compared to an equal number of drug abstainers, the latter felt much more loyalty to parents than to their friends (Coombs & Landsverk, 1988; Coombs, Paulson, & Richardson, 1991). When asked whose opinion they valued most—parents or friends—the drug-free kids consistently identified their parents.

Abstaining youth usually not only feel closer to their parents, but they consider it important to get along with them. Moreover, they aspire to be like them. Their parents usually provide plenty of praise and encouragement, win their kids' trust as well as trust their youngsters, and help their children with personal problems. Rather than ignoring parental advice, kids closely bonded with parents seek their guidance and think twice before embarrassing them with inappropriate behaviors. By contrast, drug users report more loneliness, rejection, isolation, and punishment at home.

A study of "latchkey kids" (adolescents in junior high school who are unsupervised at home after school) found that kids who are home alone two or more times per week were four times more likely to get drunk than those with parental supervision. They were also significantly more likely to smoke cigarettes or marijuana or to use inhalants (Mulhall, Stone, & Stone, 1996).

A warm relationship between father and child powerfully decreases the odds that a teen will turn to drugs. Adolescents least likely to drink and use other drugs (especially older youths) typically have close emotional ties with a male figure and receive advice and firm guidance from their mothers. Fathers who provide praise and encouragement and who play an influential role in family decisions are held in high esteem by their youngsters. "He's very understanding and easy to talk to," said one son of such a father. "He's always there for me when I need to talk to him."

Sidebar 9.1: About Fathers

Okay, dads, listen up. The key to winning the war on drugs rests not with police or laws but with you. A national survey shows that fathers who eat dinner with their children, take them to religious services, and help them with their homework greatly reduce the chances their kids will smoke, drink, or use illegal drugs. "We need a return of the family dinner in America," said Joseph Califano, Jr., president of the private National Center on Addiction and Substance Abuse at Columbia University, which conducted the study. The trouble is that most kids don't think they can turn to their dads for advice about drugs. Nearly 60 percent of the teens surveyed said their moms are easier to talk to about drugs. Only 26 percent said the same about their dads (Lessner, 1999).

Adolescents are especially vulnerable to negative family interactions. The most crushing blows to self-worth come from unsuccessful intimate relationships at home. When parents fight, complain, and criticize, youngsters withdraw from the family to protect their self-esteem. Typically they turn to friends, often those experiencing similar rejections, for acceptance. Friendships formed on this basis often lead to drug abuse and unacceptable street behaviors.

Young people's chances of receiving positive feedback from parents lessen once they start experimenting with drugs and establishing bonds with drug-using friends. Likewise, youngsters who receive positive reinforcement from drug-using peers are more likely to reject adult-imposed standards. Drug use escalates as parental impact declines and time on the streets increases.

You can best prevent this downward cycle from even beginning by avoiding negative parent-youth interaction—such as criticism and non-involvement. Establish positive interactions with your kids while they are young and hungry for your attention. If your "wake-up call" didn't come until your son or daughter became a teenager, it's not too late to start now.

Your task will be much harder, but with help you can do it. Parent training and family therapy (discussed in Part Seven) can show you how. Rather than arguing and decreeing more punishment, you will learn how to channel your anxieties and your teens' behaviors into personally beneficial and socially acceptable ways.

Sidebar 9.2: Love Supplies

Psychologist Sterling Ellsworth, Ph.D., asked people of all ages to list the ways they know they are loved. Some particularly apply to parents of teenagers:

- My parents do not need or want anything back from me.
- My parent are firm with me, and do not please me or do whatever I ask when it goes against their feelings of what is appropriate.
- I know I am loved because they listen and understand me when I talk to them. They care what I think and feel.
- They hug me, hold me, or take my hand or arm.
- They have confidence in my abilities and give me tasks to do for our family.
- They respect me. They make me feel there is something precious and beautiful inside me. It's a nonverbal thing, a certain soft look in their faces, admiration in their eyes, a certain tone in their voices, the way they sit or move.
- Their love is permanent and sure.
- They want to be with me and are happy when I'm near them.
- I know I am loved because they tell me (Ellsworth, 1995, p. 119).

Strengthening Family Bonds

Here are some recommendations to strengthen your influence.

Think Positively

Make a list of qualities you like about your offspring—and review it often. Carry it with you, adding to the list as you think of new things. You may want to give your kids a copy of this list. Most parents who seek professional help can't think of a single good characteristic at first. You can also learn to "catch" your youngsters doing praiseworthy things. Be alert for these behaviors and acknowledge them. Give kids a list of the simple things they do that please you, then express your appreciation. Encourage them to point out the good things they have done that you overlooked.

Sidebar 9.3: Cheap Love Substitutes

The following are Dr. Sterling Ellsworth's descriptions of cheap substitutes for real love supplies:

- My parents want and need something back. They may think, "I'll be hurt if you don't change."
- Their "love" is not firm. It is weak, wishy-washy, fickle, on-again-off-again, too pleasing, too nice, too polite.
- They are always right. They argue, compete, compare. They must win. They give lots of advice. They're demanding, bossy, threatening, too involved, or too concerned. I must please them by giving in.
- Physical affection turns into sex.
- Their "love" is nearly always connected with my physical appearance or performance. It is not me they really like; instead, it is an external condition, not my inner self.
- They do not really trust me. They suspect my motives; they think I will fail or sneak. They lie to me sometimes, and I have to lie to them to get along. I must hold back my real feelings. I feel trapped.
- They treat me as a possession, and their "love" is selfish. I feel used and afraid to say anything, because they'll reject me.
- One of my parents is too dependent on me. They crash if I go away or want to do something on my own. I feel obligated and responsible for their feelings. I am not free.
- My parents take me for granted. Everything comes first but me (Ellsworth, 1995, p. 119).

Be Involved and Accessible

Take time to be involved. Let your kids know how important they are to you. "My youngest son is totally into athletics," one mother reports. "I've never had any interest in athletics until he decided about age five that he lived for sports. So it became very important for me to be part of his sports life. I wanted him to know that his activities are important to me. I've tried to be his friend, share his interests and spend time together." "Whenever there's a big problem in my son's life," said a father,

> I try to be there for him. Let him know he comes first. *Just be there!* I let him know he's more important than my work or anything else. Sometimes I stay up late helping him with a school project; I try to help him by finding books or maybe fixing popcorn to get him through the night.

Compliment with a Smile

Tell your youngsters what you appreciate about them, at least once a day. Come close, smile, look them in the eye and express appreciation. This mother is unusually expressive and involved with her two sons. "Cameron [age eighteen] and I still play chase games," she reports.

> I'll hide [fully clothed] in the bathtub. My husband rolls his eyes. But when my other son, Casey, was a teenager, it was harder. He wasn't affectionate and didn't take to all the giggling and laughing. So, I put little stickers or goofy notes in his lunch every day, silly little things. It was my way of expressing love. When he graduated from high school, he took us to his locker—and there were all the stickers I'd given him, pasted all over! He saved every last one of them.

Touch

Touching is therapeutic. "When my daughters get out of sorts," a mother reports, "I ask them if they need a hug. And now my sixteen-year-old does that for me. When I'm feeling low, she'll say, 'Mom, you need a hug.' A little humor goes a long way," she explained.

"Hugs, not drugs," the slogan of one drug-prevention program, captures this principle. This may feel awkward if *your* parents didn't touch you much, but with practice, it gets easier. Keep trying. Practice until it becomes natural.

Touching is the key to this father's goodwill with his high-achieving teens. "I never pass one of them without touching," he reports.

> My boys don't always want to be hugged or kissed, but they don't mind me patting them on the fanny, or bumping into them just to tease. The girls are more willing to receive a quick hug or a squeeze on the arm—just to let them know I love them.

This is how another mother dealt with a disrespectful fifteen-year-old son who had become sullen and talked back to her.

> I had a strong feeling that I needed to hug him, to hold him tight in the rocking chair like I used to when he was little. So I pulled him over to the rocking chair and sat him on my lap. He protested and struggled but I held him tight and told him some good and happy things about himself. He relaxed and we rocked for quite some time. When his older sisters saw this, they asked how come they didn't get rocked like Ryan? So, I started doing it with them as well and they loved it.

Take Time to Listen

One study concluded that the average twelve-year-old spends only about fourteen minutes a week communicating with his or her parents. Further, twelve minutes consist primarily of reprimands and criticism. True listening looks very different. "Ever since they were little," recalled one mom, "I greeted each one with a smile at eye level, rather than looking down on them. When I disciplined, instructed, or explained some thing to them, I got down on a knee, or sat down, so that I could look them right in the eye."

When successful parents are asked for advice about how to influence their kids, most of them, like this mom, say something like, "I listen." "When I sense they are upset, I try to get them to talk, try to listen. I try hard not to give advice unless they ask for it. And that's very difficult for me."

Sidebar 9.4: Roadblocks to Listening

John Strong identifies six roadblocks to understanding what someone is really saying:

- *Just hearing the words.* We listen to the words the person is saying, but miss the point of his or her message by not understanding the feelings behind the words.
- *Defensiveness.* We hear only what we need to so we can come back with our own side of the story.
- *Waiting to talk.* We may even understand what the other person is saying, but we want to talk about ourselves. So, we just listen for a place where we can jump; for example, "That reminds me of . . ."
- *Distractions.* If we are tired, hungry, worried about something else, or late to get somewhere else, we can't listen well.
- *Closed perspective.* This is more general than being defensive. Our mind is made up beforehand about the other person and what he or she will say.
- *A need to give advice.* We try to jump right in and tell the other person what to do. This interferes with understanding what he or she is saying. Any advice we give would be ineffective, because we haven't shown that we care enough to first understand the person's feelings (Family Connections Home Learning Guide).

Listening isn't always easy, but it's a practice that pays off, as this mother of four teenagers explains:

When they come in and start talking, I try to put things down and listen. Sometimes it's hard because what they talk about bores me. When my son gives me a blow-by-blow account of the movie he just saw, it's hard to be attentive and ask interesting questions. And, I try not to preach to him. I don't like sleazy movies that contain bad language or drugs, but I don't jump all over it and scold him if he watched one. I try to listen and learn. He knows my standards and I don't need to always be the Big Judge.

Effective listening involves these skills:

- *Show you want to listen.* Face your youngster, turn yourself toward him or her. Be at a comfortable distance. Have eye contact and a pleasant, interested expression. Wait. Don't worry about the silence. It tells others that they are important enough to you that you will wait until they sort out what they want to say.
- *Don't interrupt.* When kids begin to share their feelings, don't interrupt with your own experiences or solutions. Show acceptance, interest, and warmth without judging. Say, "Oh," "I see," or "Tell me more about it." Keep the focus on your child, not on you.
- *Watch nonverbal cues.* Good listeners notice their kids' nonverbal cues—facial expressions, tone of voice, and the way they sit or stand. Ask yourself what emotions your teen's voice conveys. Does it reflect fear, hurt, excitement? Does body posture indicate that he or she is comfortable, uptight, or angry? Research suggests that people communicate more than half their messages nonverbally.
- *Check it out.* See if you understand by saying, "Do you mean . . . ?" Or, "It sounds like you are saying. . . ." Avoid asking "why" questions; they imply that the youngster needs to defend him- or herself. Use "how," "what," "where," or "who" questions instead. A good listener accepts other people's descriptions of their feelings, motives, or goals without telling them they should feel or think differently.
- *Share your perspective.* Once your kids feel that you understand, share how you see their situation. Remember, though, there is a fine line between sharing your perspective and giving advice. The difference is that you are sharing how you *see* it, rather than saying what another person should do. The other difference is that you are offering a possible alternative, not the only "right" answer. Offering alternatives helps kids gain perspective, but leaves the choice with them. Advice can be perceived as a put-down (Family Connections Home Learning Guide).

Schedule Time for Fun Together

Make it a priority to attend events your youngsters consider important. By being there, you let them know that you care and that you consider them important. Cheer for them. "If you're going to build a lifeline with your kids that will get them through a lot of challenging times," a mother explained,

> you have to do fun things with them. Spend time with your kids. That's the best way to have rapport with them. We plan activities together and go on outings and vacations. We did lots of things when they were little, but it's getting harder because now they have jobs and other activities that compete for family time.

A father observed:

> There's really no substitute for spending time with your kids if you're going to be close to them and have any kind of influence. You've got to take time to do things they're interested in. My experience is that it doesn't take a lot of time as long as it's something they like. Share with them in their excitement, make comments, and ask questions. They really like it when I'm involved with them—I've never had any success in trying to make them interested in things they don't like.

A family's strength is equal to the ratio of its positive to negative interactions. That is, healthy families have a lot of positive encounters (smiling, touching, listening, praising, doing fun activities together, and giving time, small favors, and other gifts) and they avoid negative ones (abandonment, criticism, complaining, reprimands, ignoring, and emotional aloofness). Make the highest priority in your family to increase the positives and reduce the negatives. All your other life achievements will pale in comparison to the satisfaction of warm, caring relationships with family members.

Whereas other people pass through our lives like ships at sea, family members are permanent. Do all you can to cherish them, to build friendships during their developmental years. A counselor at a residential program for wayward youth remarked:

> It's my philosophy that parents need to establish early in a child's life their desire to be with them. When they hit thirteen or thereabouts and want to be with their peers, you won't have much influence unless they've already experienced a lot of good times with you. After that you begin competing with their friends, so unless you've established a pretty good relationship with them, it's pretty hard to get them to want to be with you. It's critical that you establish fun relationships with them early on in life so that they want to continue doing that in their teens.

He cited this rare example:

> I know one father who spends so much time having fun with his kids that his teenagers would rather be home than out with their friends. They laugh, let

their hair down, and have a wonderful time. They are so close as a family that the peers don't carry much weight.

ACTIVITIES FOR PARENTS AND KIDS

9.1 What "love supplies" make each person in your family feel loved and appreciated? You might post a list on the refrigerator. Commit to providing love supplies for each other. After a trial-run week, discuss how well you did as a family and how you might continue and/or improve your efforts (Ellsworth, 1995, p. 119).

9.2 Once a week, pick a family member and have everyone share the three qualities they like about that person. The individual listens and makes one of three replies: "Thank you," "Thank you, I agree," or "Thank you, tell me more." Another time, each family member can take turns sharing the three accomplishments or challenges they've met that they're particularly proud of. Other family members can admire their growth and learn a little more about what matters most to them. This works well at New Year's or birthdays (Family Connections Home Learning Guide, n.d.).

9.3 Schedule a family-activity night every one to two weeks (at least once a month). At dinner or during a family council meeting, the family can vote on, schedule, and plan activities: expeditions to the library, zoo, park, or movies, or a night of board games, dancing, or ice-cream sundaes at home. Perhaps a different family member can pick the activity each time, with other family members agreeing to cooperate.

9.4 Busy families are involved in lots of activities outside the home. In addition, friends, relatives, teachers, physicians, and others play a role in the family's well-being. To keep things running smoothly, have a system for keeping track of who's doing what. (See Appendix C.)

REFERENCES

Coombs, Robert H., & John Landsverk. 1988. "Parenting Style and Substance Use During Childhood and Adolescence." *Journal of Marriage and the Family*, 50(2), May, pp. 473–482.

Coombs, Robert H., John Landsverk, & Mark A. Richardson. 1991. "Peer versus Parental Influence in Substance Use Among Hispanic and Anglo Children and Adolescents." *Journal of Youth and Adolescence*, 20(1), pp. 73–88.

Ellsworth, Sterling G. 1995. *How I Got This Way and What to Do about It*. 3153 Metolius Drive, Eugene, OR 97408.

Family Connections Home Learning Guide, Utah State University Extension, n.d.

Lessner, Lori. 1999. "Involved Dads Help Keep Kids Off Drugs." *Daily News*, August 31, pp. 1, 8.

Mulhall, P. F., D. Stone, & B. Stone. 1996. "Home Alone. Is It A Risk Factor for Middle School Youth and Drug Use?" *Journal of Drug Education*, 26(1), pp. 39–48.

CHAPTER

10 Set Limits Without Using Anger or Authoritarian Methods

Adolescents who clearly understand parental expectations about alcohol and other drugs are much more likely to avoid using them. Such parents might tell their child, "We love you. Your health and safety are important to us. So if a person offers you beer, wine, or any other type of alcoholic drink, we want you to say no."

Parental Standards

One study of drug-using and abstaining teens shows that abstainers' parents have firmer standards regarding curfew, television, schoolwork, and use of alcohol and other drugs (Coombs & Landsverk, 1990). To make your parental control as effective as possible, develop unambiguous expectations of your kids and then praise them when they meet them. "We have some simple things we decided on in our family," a father reported,

> and all the kids know they apply to everyone; nothing personal, they all have the same limits. They include homework, curfew, helping out with chores—just old-fashioned things. We don't allow swearing in our home or opposite-sex friends in their bedrooms. We don't leave it up to our kids to enforce these rules with their friends; we tell them directly: "Here's our family rules, stick with them. Okay?"

> Some parents link TV and driving privileges with achievement. "During school nights the TV in our home doesn't go on until everybody's homework is done. It's a sacrifice for the parents as well as the kids, but it's worth it; they're all good students."
> The family profile of youthful abstainers shows parents playing an active role in setting limits, providing counsel and advice, and offering trust and encouragement. Rather than resorting to emotional outbursts and harsh

punishment, these parents influence their children by clarifying appropriate behaviors.

Sidebar 10.1: Firm Touch

Sometimes a calm touch will ensure compliance from youngsters. On a scout trip, a twelve-year-old boy refused for the third time to move into his assigned vehicle. "All the boys were watching and I wondered what would happen," a mother reports. "Jim [the scoutmaster] put his arm around the boy's shoulder and gently led him to the proper vehicle. He didn't yell or threaten him. The boy just needed a firm physical touch."

It's easy to coerce young children into behaving. Dictatorial methods— yelling, spanking, judging, criticizing—may work at the time, but they also lead to alienation and hostility. Listening, negotiating, and talking things through calmly let kids maintain their dignity and strengthen parent-child friendship. Knee-jerk reactions like yelling and screaming undermine this rapport, as this letter to a father from a twenty-year-old son living abroad illustrates:

> The people I'm working with yell and hit their kids and then wonder why their kids scream and hit back when they're adults. I remember you were generally very calm in times of high tension. You told me once you didn't do any disciplining while you were angry, but would wait until you cooled off so you wouldn't say or do things you later regretted. Remember the night I told you that my friend Matt had erased all the memory on your computer? I guess that was reason enough for you to get upset—but you didn't explode. Sure, I was later forbidden to use the computer, but I was too scared to use it anyway. I felt miserable about it. Even in times of stress, you kept peace in our home.

Parents (especially fathers) of youthful drug users are more likely to be emotionally distant. Mothers in these homes are less trusting and firm, and fathers play a scant role in family decisions and discussions about personal problems and future plans. When asked about her home life as a child, an ex-addict responds, "I didn't like it. Ever since I was twelve, my mother let me do whatever I wanted. It was like not really having anyone around who cared about me. She never really disciplined me." As children become older, parents, especially fathers, increasingly need to clarify behavioral expectations and provide abundant positive rewards when youngsters meet them.

Sidebar 10.2: Teens and Dads

Parenting Teens' monthly newsletter offers tips for fathers who want to stay in touch with their teens:

- Listen, don't lecture.
- Respect your teens' right to their opinion, even if it differs from yours.
- Hug them, even if they pull away.
- Believe in them, regardless of their grade-point average or athletic abilities.
- Organize activities for you and your kids or with other dads and teens.
- Establish rituals that are uniquely yours, such as cooking Saturday-morning breakfast or going for a run together.
- Get support from other dads.
- Don't hold your teens to a higher standard of behavior than you hold yourself.
- Don't try to change your teens. Let them be who they are, not who you think they should be.
- Pick your battles. Save your efforts for issues that involve safety or morals.

For further information on how to be a more involved father, visit these Web sites:

American Coalition for Fathers and Children: www.acfc.org
Center for Successful Fathering: www.fathering.org
Dads Can: www.dadscan.org
National Center for Fathering: www.fathers.com
National Fatherhood Initiative: www.fatherhood.org

(Jackson, 2000, p. 3.)

As an out-of-control teenager, TV host Oprah Winfrey was sent to live with her father. "I was a child who was always in need of discipline," she recalled. "I was definitely headed for a career as a juvenile delinquent." A strict but always kind disciplinarian, he meant what he said—and Oprah knew it! "I knew exactly what I could and couldn't get away with," she recalled. "I *respected* his authority. . . . It's because of him, I believe, I am where I am today" (Adler, 1997).

Being frank with teens about parental expectations comes easily for some parents. "When it comes to the-birds-and-the-bees talk, I don't pull any punches," said a mother.

When my sons start dating these voluptuous young ladies, I tell them, "I don't want you to have to go talk to the father of some girl that you've gotten pregnant. You don't want that responsibility and neither do I, so you better behave yourself. If you think you're not able to control yourself, I'll sew your fly shut!" They think that's funny, but it gets the message across.

This is how another mother involves her teenagers in setting behavioral expectations and then makes them accountable: "When they go out on weekends, I ask, 'Now what's a reasonable time for you to be home?'" And when they return, she asks more questions. "When my kids come in they have to kiss me goodnight; that's always been the rule. And then we talk. 'What did you do?' 'Where did you go?' 'Who did you see?' I ask a bunch of questions until they want me to quit!"

What's the big deal about keeping family rules? Trust. "I had an all-pro daughter when it came to breaking the curfew agreement," reports a dad.

> I explained to her that if she continually broke our agreements we couldn't trust her. I tried to teach her that keeping agreements builds trust. We didn't give her much slack or latitude until she regained our trust. She knew she had to abide by our rules to get privileges. It took her a long time but eventually she learned—the hard way.

What happens when kids are not trustworthy? "My kids like me to trust them and they get real angry and defensive when I don't," said one mother. "It's really hard, but sometimes I just have to say it. 'I really don't trust you right now. I've had several indications things aren't going well—your judgment isn't good—so as your parent, I have to step in and help you.'"

Sidebar 10.3: Temper Your Temper

Try these techniques for controlling your anger:

- *Mentally step back.* Often it's the little things that push people's buttons, such as children making too much noise. When you find yourself growing angry, mentally separate yourself from the situation and ask yourself whether it really deserves a dramatic response. Remind yourself of what really matters in life—doing good work, being happy, and nurturing your children. These factors are more important than getting mad—or getting even.
- *Create a moment of calm.* Take a deep breath, hold it for a moment, and as you slowly let it out, tell yourself, *This can't be the biggest problem in the world today.*
- *Move around.* When you find yourself getting angry, walk around, run up and down the stairs, or jog in place. Physical movement helps to dilute adrenaline and other chemicals that fuel anger, and it triggers the release of calming endorphins. Exercising every day

(not only when you're angry) reduces tension and provides time for you to think about and make peace with what's bothering you.

■ *Eliminate "should."* People with anger problems tend to have strong feelings about how others *should* behave. Rather than judging people for doing things you don't like, pretend you're just an observer. Drop your expectations about what *should* happen. If you don't judge, you won't get angry.

■ *Make yourself smile.* When you force yourself to smile—even when you don't feel like doing it—you experience a rapid decrease in stress hormones and an increase in calming endorphins.

■ *Defuse with humor.* Rather than getting caught up in the emotions of the moment, try to find something funny in the situation. Like exercise, humor reduces the physical arousal caused by anger and distracts you until you can think more clearly.

■ *Put yourself in control.* Rather than telling yourself, *That guy is making me furious,* turn it around and say, *I'm getting angry at that guy.* By shifting emphasis, you take responsibility for your own anger, which puts you in control. People who feel powerful are less likely to get angry.

■ *Discuss what's bothering you.* People who never talk about what bothers them eventually explode. When something bothers you, say so. Explain your view in a polite, reasonable way, without getting nasty or aggressive.

■ *Look for solutions.* Anger never solves problems. If anything, it makes people do things that escalate situations. Finding solutions to what's bothering you puts you in control of the situation (McKee, 2000, pp. 7–8).

When kids don't obey family rules, act decisively, but not with anger. "I never say, 'Wait 'til your father gets home,'" a mother reports. "He doesn't want them to be afraid of him, so when my son starts something, I finish it." Another mother of six explained,

> I don't like to give my kids an opportunity to lie to me. I don't ask, "Where were you last night?" when I know full well where they were. One was at the house of a friend whose parents were out of town—I already knew that—so I told her I knew. "What's the deal?", I asked her. "What were you thinking?" I let her explain herself and tried to keep her from lying or being on the defensive.

The mother of a rebellious teenager refused to give up when her daughter would not comply with curfew rules.

> I picked her up at one a.m. and she informed me that I was ruining her life— none of the other girls had a curfew. She pouted all the way home and later on

slipped out to return to the party. I was furious when I found her gone and went back to the party in nothing but my red nightgown and slippers; I didn't take the time to get dressed. After about fifteen minutes of knocking on the window, her friends begged her to stop me, so she finally came out. I was quite an embarrassment to her and I thought she would never talk to me again.

Later on she told me how much she appreciated me coming to get her. Although she ended up losing the prize football player to a rival, she was glad she didn't have to pay the required price. I think our kids are crying out for us to enforce some boundaries. Her friends still tease me about it, but I don't regret it for a moment. Who knows what I saved her from that night!

While kids may not like their parents to "sweat the little stuff," most are grateful when parents care enough to come to their aid when they are self-destructing. "My dad is lenient with me on the little things, like forgetting to make my bed," a seventeen-year-old son said, "but gets very upset over the big things, like cheating in school or stealing."

Encouraging Compliance

Here are specific suggestions:

Family Meetings

Hold a regular monthly family meeting for thirty to forty-five minutes to schedule events and negotiate problems and issues. Start the meeting with something fun. Draw up a family constitution, decide what specific behaviors you can reasonably expect, and list the consequences for deviating from these guidelines. Consistently fine-tune these rules to fit with your experiences and changing family circumstances. In this meeting, discuss your family position on alcohol and other drugs. Although you organize these meetings, encourage your youngsters to do most of the talking. Basic rules for this meeting are (1) everyone who wants to gets a chance to talk—one at a time, (2) it's okay to say what you feel and, (3) no one may interrupt or put anyone else down. End the meeting with refreshments.

Daily Connections

Gather together regularly each day as a family, preferably at the evening meal. If you make this a priority, it will help keep you closer and up-to-date on potential problems and issues. Ask questions and *listen*. Try not to dominate.

"My parents and I had a pretty open relationship," a young adult recalled. He credited this openness with keeping him anchored to home values when most of his peers were going off in opposite directions.

They really encouraged me to ask questions. I never remember a question that I felt ashamed to ask. They were very family centered. We regularly connected with each other as a family over dinner. This gave us a chance to share stuff and to work through painful issues—like sexuality.

One father asked each of his kids to come to dinner with a current event from the newspaper. "Our dinnertime conversations were always interesting and put us all on the same level," he recalled. "It was very easy for them to bring up whatever was going on at school, in society, questions about sex and drugs—things like that."

Control of Anger

Control your anger when provoked by offensive youthful behavior. Follow these steps:

1. *Wait!* Anger isn't a permanent state; it will fade, so don't express yourself immediately. Take time to cool down and reflect. Go for a walk to let off some steam and then approach the problem calmly. Recognize that the object of your anger is a circumstance, an event, or a behavior, *not* the person you love. "My mom set the timer in her kitchen for ten minutes whenever she became angry and exasperated with me," recalled a young adult now successful in his new marriage and career. She cooled off during this time and then discussed the problem without making things worse.

2. *Use "I" not "you" language.* Rather than using an attack approach— "*You* said this or "*You* did that" (which only causes defensiveness and belligerence)—simply state how *you* feel ("*I* feel [this] when you do [that]"). Express yourself in four sentences or less. Practice by writing it down first and saying it to yourself several times before you address your kids.

3. *Be ready to listen* to rationalizations and excuses, but don't counter with arguments. Just listen until emotions are diffused. Mutual rules and objectives can be calmly defined. If the same problematic behavior occurs again, put it on the agenda for the family council meeting. Don't try to justify yourself; such defensiveness will undermine your authority and probably lead to an argument. You need only relate your feelings.

Set Boundaries for TV and Internet Viewing

TV watching in the United States remains high, with most children under eleven watching nearly twenty hours per week. "We have the most sedentary generation of young people in American history," U.S. Surgeon General David Satcher said. "Reducing the amount of television our children watch is one way to encourage more healthful activity" ("New Diet for Kids: Lose the TV," 1999).

"In retrospect," said a mom,

I wish I had not allowed my son to have a TV in his own room. It became impossible to keep him from staying up late watching it, and it caused a lot of problems. Tell parents to never, never let their children have a TV in their room because it will hurt their chances of getting through school, adjusting work schedules, having a good social life, and feeling good, and make them more prone to depression and other problems—all of which increase the odds of their becoming involved with drugs. A TV turn-off time can't be enforced if it's in the kids' bedroom.

Sidebar 10.4: TV Grip on Kids

"In a wired world, TV still has a grip on kids," notes Brian Lowry, staff writer for the *Los Angeles Times*. ". . . television's ability to galvanize kids remains unshaken despite competition from Internet Age technologies. . . .

"With computers, the Internet, video games, and other technologies vying for their leisure time and attention, kids appear to be consuming more media of all kinds. Many are 'multitasking,' watching TV and surfing the Internet at the same time, for example. Statistical Research Inc. (SRI), a media-analysis firm in Westfield, New Jersey, has also been monitoring children's media habits, interviewing kids between the ages of eight and seventeen about media usage. More than half the kids polled said they have television sets in their rooms, and two-thirds reported that their TV time overlaps other activities. . . .

"Some advocates concerned about TV's influence are, not surprisingly, disturbed by these latest findings. 'When kids are spending three hours a day in front of the TV, they don't have time to read; they don't have time to go outside,' noted Jennifer Kurz of TV Turnoff Network, which urges people to watch less television and sponsors an annual turn-off-the-TV week. Given the data chronicling greater TV usage, 'we have our work cut out for us,' Kurz conceded" (Lowry, 2000, pp. F1, F11).

If you have concerns about what your kids see on the Internet—there's lots of raunchy stuff mixed in with highly valuable programs—you may want to install a cable leading from their computer to a second monitor screen in the kitchen or living room. Then you (from another part of the house) can see whatever your child views. Sound like Big Brother? How is this any different from deciding what books are in your children's library, or ensuring that they don't see morally degrading movies? If you don't like this approach, think of something else. There's too much at stake for you to adopt a *laissez-faire* attitude. (See Appendices D and E for Internet safety tips and a listing of available blocking and filtering software.)

ACTIVITIES FOR PARENTS AND KIDS

10.1 Agree on a "cool-off" code word for times when tempers get out of control. Agree that if anyone uses the code word, both parties will schedule a time to meet to discuss the problem more calmly.

10.2 Negotiate family contracts. Ask kids to write down what they think you should expect of them (and why) in the areas of homework, curfew, clean-up, money, use of the car, and drugs and alcohol. They should also list possible consequences for not meeting standards. Meanwhile, write down what you think you should expect of them and why. Also list consequences. Discuss your lists to negotiate an acceptable compromise. (If children are reluctant to accept any expectations, explain that the only reason you would let them run wild in this crazy world is if you didn't care about them—and you do, very, very much. Then try again.)

10.3 Have each family member choose a situation below, and write down how they would reach a decision on it and what they would do. Then, listen to others' points of view.

Problem 1: Friday night is the big game with your school's rival school. It is also your cousin's wedding. You want to go to both. What do you do?

Problem 2: You have $25. You see the perfect sweater that will match several other articles of clothing you have. It is also just one week before your mother's birthday. You don't have enough money to buy a gift *and* the sweater. What do you do?

Problem 3: You've been asked to join the track team for spring season. You also want to be in the school play. Both play rehearsal and team practice are at the same time after school. What do you do?

10.4 Read about family councils in Appendix F and implement a plan.

REFERENCES

Adler, Bill, editor. 1997. *The Uncommon Wisdom of Oprah Winfrey: A Portrait in Her Own Words.* London: Aurum.

Coombs, Robert H., & John Landsverk. 1988. "Parenting Styles and Substance Use During Childhood and Adolescence." *Journal of Marriage and the Family,* 50(2), May, pp. 473–482.

Jackson, Karla. 2000. "Family Matters." *The Tampa Tribune,* March 18, p. 3.

Lowry, Brian. 2000. "In Wired World, TV Still Has Grip on Kids." *Los Angeles Times,* September 18, pp. F1, F11.

McKee, Michael G. 2000. "Simple Ways to Temper Your Temper . . . and Turn Your Anger into a Constructive Force." *Bottom Line,* July 15, pp. 7–8.

"New Diet for Kids: Lose the TV," May 5, 1999, from www.channel2000.com.

11 Provide Opportunities for Success Experiences

You are in a pivotal position to provide your children with natural "highs"—rewarding, adventurous, drug-free experiences that will help them become successful adults. "If I were to give advice to parents," said one parent educator, "I'd say, 'Make sure your kids feel capable, significant, and influential. Help them have success experiences every single day and be actively involved in decision-making.'"

Sidebar 11.1: Family Facilitator

"I make clear," said a parent, "that I'm willing to sacrifice for music lessons or any other kind of self-improvement. I'm there for them. I'm willing to drive them anywhere they need to go. If they need to get to school to work out, they know they can get a ride."

Enhancing Skills and Confidence

Providing activities that build skills and confidence is one of the most important things you can do for your children, especially during their junior and senior high school years. This includes:

1. helping to structure free time that otherwise might be idle;
2. promoting skills and knowledge in activities that develop confidence. Examples include athletic activities, adventures (e.g., wilderness challenge courses), creative or artistic activities, and community-center involvements such as Boys and Girls Clubs; and
3. providing community-service opportunities. (See Chapter 16.) Most important, make your own life a model for them. "If your example

doesn't back up your words," a father observed, "you're not going to have much influence at home."

> If you want kids to read good books, read good books. If you want them to be active rather than sit around watching TV, be active yourself. If you want them to love good music, play good music at home when they're little. We buy a lot of sound tracks from popular movies and kids' shows. Most of it is pretty good, and we play it a lot. Every now and then [the kids] turn on something classical. A neighbor's mouth dropped open in amazement when Mike came in from working in the yard, opened all the windows, and put on the *1812 Overture* at full volume.

Facilitate their success. "I try to identify some area where my kids have strength socially and build on that," a mother remarked.

> For instance, Elaine loves to read and she remembers things so well. When she was in junior high school, I pointed out how interesting and witty she was as a conversationalist. I told her that she'd attract people because she shares so easily. When she started dating, I told her she'd have nothing to worry about; guys would love being with her. She's very confident now.

Help your son or daughter become involved in activities that develop skills, or talents that will bring personal enjoyment and recognition from others. Creative activities like art, drama, and music bring satisfaction to some youths. Others enjoy big-muscle activities that involve adventure and sports.

Sidebar 11.2: Happy Memories

"When I was a kid, my parents didn't have that much money for things like closets full of the latest clothes. I realize now they spent any extra they had on lessons and activities. I remember taking art lessons, swimming lessons, dance lessons, and various music lessons including piano, clarinet, and voice. Over the years, I was able to participate in school orchestras and bands, which gave me a social spot even though I was not that popular. My sisters were on city soccer teams. I was more up for outdoor sports, and my parents got me in a coed scout troop led by my high school Spanish teacher, a man we all looked up to. We went camping and rafting, things like that. I also got to go on various youth expeditions with my church, including hiking in the High Sierras and in Robbers' Roost, where Butch Cassidy and the Sundance Kid used to hide out. I'd say that all made up for my lack of designer clothing in junior high."

One father did some careful planning to encourage academic success.

One of my sons was highly motivated and needed no help. I didn't have to say boo to him. But the others would wiggle out of their homework. So I set up a space in the family room, a table with supplies, and all the reference books they might need. They would all sit there and work on their homework until it was completed. They liked being together.

Involve yourself in your child's school activities. "I've been on all my son's sports teams' committees," a mom reports. "Whether as a fund-raiser or a telephone person or a team mother, I'm involved with the team." "My kids never played a ballgame without someone there cheering for them," another commented. "Baseball, football, soccer, I was there. If we went on vacation and couldn't come, we asked Grandma or Grandpa or the older kids to be there for us. Oftentimes, all three brothers would show up."

Here's another success story:

My daughter used to seek the popular in-crowd at school, but she made a decision to seek out friends who were not the big shots—this was better for her. She started a Thursday-night bowling league where *everyone* was welcome. She ended up with twenty or thirty kids who all had great fun together. They always stopped before eleven thirty p.m. because she had to be home by then. She learned how to have fun with a group that was safe. There was no way to teach her this except by giving her the tools to understand that when she was with a crowd that did the wrong things, she would eventually be pulled down with the peer pressure. It had happened to her before. Today she is one of the most fantastic women I know.

If you are a single parent and can't be home to organize and supervise after-school activities, look into out–of-school programs. More than a "safe place to go," these programs must fit the interests and needs of young people. Milbrey McLaughlin, professor of education at Stanford University, has had more than twelve years of conversations with twelve-to-eighteen-year-old kids in challenging circumstances. She reports that kids do better in school and life when they're involved in out-of-school programs that provide exciting learning. In her report *Community Counts: How Youth Organizations Matter for Youth Development,* McLaughlin states that kids who participate in after-school programs achieve higher academic levels and have higher expectations for themselves; demonstrate greater self-confidence and optimism about what the future holds; express a strong desire to "give back" to their communities; and become more productive, employed, and active members of their communities (www.jointogether.org).

Exercise, Service, and Reading Activities

Three activities merit special mention: athletics, service, and reading. Exercise benefits kids' overall mental health. Young people who exercise vigorously usually feel good during and after their exercise and experience a sense of calmness and reduced stress. Physically active kids are often happier and healthier than sedentary ones, as this father recalled:

Volleyball saved two of my daughters in high school after they experimented with a crowd who smoked marijuana and drank. Practicing after school and participating in weekend tournaments kept them really busy and tired. I went with them to all their tournaments and I tried to keep the communication lines open. This was easy for me because I love sports and loved to watch my girls play, and I praised them extensively! It has created a very special bond between us that continues to this day. I think it saved us a lot of would-be tragedies.

Evidence also shows that kids benefit emotionally and physically by helping others. Altruism builds happiness in at least two ways: It helps make young people feel good about themselves, and it relieves physical and mental stress, thereby enhancing health and happiness.

You will be surprised how much young children can enjoy and benefit from helping activities. Without your encouragement, involvement, and guidance, it is unlikely that they will experience these altruistic highs. Your investment in these activities will do wonders for them in their formative years and pay major dividends later. (More about this in Chapter 16.)

Sidebar 11.3: Three Generations of Readers

When I was a kid, my dad took my brother and sister and me to the public library almost every Saturday morning. It was great for us and later I realized that it also gave my mom a break. We could stay almost as long as we wanted and check out as many books as we desired. Dad sat in the children's section and consulted with us about which books to get. He sometimes read to the youngest. All those books were riches at our fingertips. So much available and we didn't need any money. I remember sitting on the rug reading some of the books to see if I really wanted to check them out. Were they good enough to take home to read again? My dad made a big production of each of us getting our own library card when we were old enough.

When I became a mother, I, too, took my children to the library every week. Each child took a plastic dishpan to bring home the books. I enjoyed looking through the shelves of children's books to help them pick favorites. Once a librarian commented that I seemed to find the best books. We read to our children almost daily until into their teens. One of our children says reading together is one of her best childhood memories. Another daughter collects, writes, and publishes children's books.

Now that all our children are grown, we enjoy exchanging books and talking about what we've read.

Thanks, Dad!

Cultivate in your child a love of good books. This will provide a lifetime of pleasure and open the doors of understanding, opportunity, and success. Whatever time and energy you invest in reading with your child will yield results like compound interest on a financial investment. One that loves reading has everything within their grasp.

A family reading program not only increases success opportunities for children, it strengthens emotional bonds with them as well. Anyone who has been read to during their childhood and adolescence remembers with fondness those special times.

Sidebar 11.4: Encourage Reading

- Make wholesome, interesting reading available.
- Set an example by reading yourself.
- Help your kids start their own libraries and swap books with friends.
- Take them to the library regularly to check out all they want.
- Take them to used book stores, sort through the collection, and purchase one or two that capture kids' interests.
- No matter what their age, read to them (ask your librarians for suggestions).
- Relax bedtime rules weekends; let your kids stay up as late as they want as long as they're reading in bed.
- Hold D-E-A-R (Drop Everything and Read) times when everyone in the family sits down for uninterrupted reading time.

Set aside a specific time for reading every day, such as immediately following the family meal or right before bedtime. These are times for the family to be together, so everyone can share the experience and discuss what they've read.

Next, find suitable reading materials. When selecting a book, consider the choice with great care, as many books open visions of understanding and delight. Thumb through the book and check the contents, not just the advertising hype on the dust jacket. When selecting fiction, choose a book with a compelling storyline, something that will capture your child's interest and give him or her something to think about. Books such as *Where the Red Fern Grows, Summer of the Monkeys*, or the James Herriot books (e.g., *All Things Bright and Beautiful*) are excellent choices.

Biographies are great. Select books related to your child's own personal interests, such as airplanes, rock-climbing, and so forth. This will not only encourage discussion, it will increase your ability to understand your son or daughter. And they will learn that books contain a wealth of ideas, wisdom, and fun. In the pages of a good book, your child can dream, form ideas, and come away with valued memories.

Ask others for book recommendations. There are people who can help you select high quality books and they are usually eager to help you. Start with your local librarian or your child's school teacher, and collect lists of good books, such as the acclaimed Newberry Award Books.

If you think your son or daughter is too old for this, or too involved with TV and friends, think again. Involve them in setting a family reading goal and in selecting the books. If you read out loud from a good book each day, they'll come to love the experience. And take them to the library to browse and choose books for their own personal reading.

ACTIVITIES FOR PARENTS AND KIDS

11.1 As a family, research local opportunities to participate in theater, musical, sports, service, or other activities—then sign up for a few! Does your community center or college offer inexpensive art or dance classes? Try new things. Be bold!

11.2 Have each family member write down a definition of "success" and list at least three times they felt successful. (If someone can't think of any, other family members can help him or her brainstorm.) Share what you've written. Then discuss the following quotation: "I have lived simply, laughed frequently, and loved deeply. I am a success."

11.3 Send your mind on brief vacations. Researchers say the body responds in similar ways to something you vividly imagine as it does to something that actually happens. Often this works against us, we create stress by worrying about what *might* happen in the future, or we regret what happened in the past. But our thoughts and imaginations can work *for us* as well. Thinking about pleasant experiences, or imagining being in a restful place, can reduce stress. Here's what to do:

   a. When your family is situated comfortably, and the radio, television, and phone are turned off, give the following instructions. "I want you to picture in your mind a favorite place where you were happy and had especially good feelings about yourself and life. (Pause.) Were there any smells that you remember? What do you remember hearing? What were the temperature and the weather like? Try to remember how it looked as clearly as you can."

b. After giving family members a few moments to fix their memory clearly in their minds, ask who would like to share their memory. Give everyone a turn to share.

c. Discuss what made these experiences especially happy ones. Describe how it makes you feel to remember and talk about them now.

d. Encourage family members to periodically practice visiting this favorite place in their minds. When they're feeling depressed or stressed, a brief mental vacation can give them a boost (*Family Connections Home Learning Guide*, n.d.).

11.4 Encourage your kids to read biographies of people they admire and to keep a list of those books. What traits make others successful? Discuss at the dinner table.

REFERENCES

Family Connections Home Learning Guide, Utah State University Extension, n.d.
Parents Make the Difference! 2000. From: www.par-inst.com/resources/44ideas.

INTERNET SOURCES

www.theantidrug.com
www.jointogether.org

12 Establish Meaningful Family Activities and Traditions

Imagine yourself a few years from now looking back on the good times you had with your family—enjoyable activities that you did together with laughter and delight. What might you add to this list, and how can you get started? Doing things together isn't an obligation—it's your most valuable opportunity to protect your kids from drugs and other hazards!

Family Fun

When asked, "What makes a happy family?" children usually respond, "Doing things together." With work pressures always present and TV readily available, it is easy to miss out on family fun. Healthy families make a conscious effort to plan activities that they can do together. And these activities need not be elaborate or expensive.

Make family fun a high priority. Mutually rewarding activities between kids and their parents strengthen interpersonal bonds and enhance parental influence. One family teases their mom because she is always bringing new games home for them to play together. Undaunted, she persists, knowing that the fun they share holds them together.

Sidebar 12.1: Activities with Kids

- Encourage kids to play on a sports team—then cheer for them.
- Arrange for a game of "Capture the Flag."
- Take youngsters to a driving range to hit golf balls.
- Participate in nature walks together.
- Hold a monthly swimming and pizza day.
- Get season passes to the local minor-league baseball team.
- Establish an annual family minigolf tournament.
- Help kids build a soap-box car and then hold a derby.
- Build a skateboard park for kids.

- Take them bowling.
- Take them canoeing down a nearby river.
- Schedule an "Adventure Day" to explore someplace new.
- Organize a water-balloon fight.
- Coordinate a scavenger hunt.
- Install a basketball hoop and play together.
- Take your teens horseback riding.
- Visit state parks and take guided hikes.
- Take them camping, even if only in the backyard.
- Go to a nearby amusement park.
- Play flashlight tag on a warm night.
- Schedule a family game night.
- Help kids set up an obstacle course.
- Make homemade ice cream together.
- Coordinate a weekly Family Film Festival.
- Create and tend an ant farm together.
- Pick strawberries together at a local farm.
- Organize a neighborhood block party.
- Organize a chili cook-off party.
- Arrange a tour of a fire station/pizza parlor/donut shop (www. theantidrug.com).

Here are some other suggestions: In addition to your monthly family council, hold a weekly family-planning meeting to schedule activities. Encourage your children's suggestions and mark these dates on a common calendar. (See Appendix C.)

Family activities might include an annual family vacation (especially if everyone is involved in the planning and preparations), creation of a photo album to relive all the fun experiences, or a weekly activity night of sports, games, singing, dancing, and telling stories. Keep the television off and ignore the telephone during these evenings. Encourage fun and offer special refreshments. Above all, don't lecture anyone.

Sidebar 12.2 : Family Vacations

"When I was little, we used to cross the desert every summer in an old turquoise station wagon to visit our relatives. My brother and sister and I would play the alphabet word-search game with billboards and license plates when we weren't singing or bickering or snoozing. When we finally got there, we played with our cousins in my grandmother's backyard while the grown-ups talked. My grandmother had this big tree we liked to climb. We all fit up there!

"Later our family started going to Sequoia National Park in the summer. We stayed in old cabins with wood-burning stoves where we scrambled eggs with potatoes and onions. We hiked everywhere, we craned our necks to look up at the giant trees, we splashed in the river, and we ran shrieking whenever a bear wandered through camp. Those times are probably my best childhood memories."

Another regular activity might be a monthly evening out for one parent and each child. It doesn't have to be expensive—just a bike ride, a ball game, a dinner out, or a walk—whatever is enjoyable for both of you. Get better acquainted. Let the conversation flow naturally. You'll find that it's much easier to talk freely when you're engaged together in an enjoyable activity. Make planning and implementing these fun times an important agenda item during your family council meetings. Always have something fun to look forward to.

Family Traditions

Family traditions also strengthen family bonds. Which traditions brought you delight as a child—waffles on Sunday morning, coloring Easter eggs, Passover Seder, making special cookies for the neighbors on holidays? Keep these traditions alive and institute new ones. For example, on birthdays and other special occasions, recognize your youngster with a red plate at the dinner table. A father explains,

> Our society moves so fast that nothing seems permanent or solid. So it's important that our kids have some traditions that endure, and it anchors them as they start their own families. They take these traditions with them to remind them of who they are and where they came from.

Sidebar 12.3: Family Traditions

"Every spring, the first beautiful warm day, whether the weatherman says it is spring or not, we fly Styrofoam planes. They are inexpensive, between $2 and $4 at Wal-Mart, and provide lots of exercise and fun and don't require a lot of adult supervision. We found a new type of plane to fly this year as well. It is called an "AirHog." It is a propeller-driven Styrofoam plane that uses compressed air to power the real piston engine. You dock the plane to a pump and fill the pressure tank with air by pumping it up like you would a bike tire. When the pressure gauge says you're ready, you let it go and watch it fly and chase it! Also remember to take a jug of water, even watching makes you thirsty" (www. loveathome.com/traditions/trd04.html).

One mother keeps a personal journal for each of her children.

I started when they were little because they would say the cutest things. I got each of them a journal and started writing all these things down. They are absolutely priceless and help us all keep a perspective on our lives and what's important. Some Sunday afternoons we get them out and look at the pictures they've drawn and remember all the sweet things they've said and done.

Sidebar 12.4: Birthday Traditions

"Our family traditionally has a big party for each person's birthday. A few years ago we started a new tradition: At the party, we go around the table and each one in turn says something nice about or for the birthday person. We vary it each year. One year we each said two things we liked about the birthday person. Another time we tried to predict what would happen to that person in the next five years. Another time we shared memories, and last year we each told two wishes we'd give them if we had unlimited magic power. It puts the entire focus on the birthday person. Everybody loves it and it brings us closer together."

Family traditions often continue from generation to generation. "We have a Sunday-dinner tradition just like my mother did," a mom said. "I fix a really good meal and all my kids who live nearby come (even roommates) as well as the invalid lady next door. I like that tradition, and it's now going into the third generation."

Holidays offer the ideal opportunity to develop some family traditions. "We have a Christmas tradition," said a mother. "Each year every kid got their own ornament, and when they get married they take them to place on their own family tree." Another mom reports,

The day before Thanksgiving we make pies, any kind they want. I get all the ingredients and everybody works together. Last year we made nineteen. We have a lot of fun. One year my two teenage kids made thirty cherry cheesecake pies and gave them all away. It made them feel good.

"When the kids were little, I bought some inexpensive toy guns that shoot little ping-pong balls, and we had a mock fight," said a father.

Every year now they look in their stocking for the toys and a fight quickly ensues. It was a great ice-breaker between them and their new stepmother— better than anything I could have devised. We still find balls from past years under the furniture. And when we do, we remember all the fun of running throughout the whole house shooting each other, screaming, and falling down. It's been a lot of fun.

You may be wondering how you can find the time and energy to add these extra meetings and activities to your already full schedule. Here's how: Simply turn off the television set. Studies show that the typical person spends nearly half of his or her leisure time watching television, more than two hours per day, the equivalent of seven years over the course of a lifetime. One study showed that the children of heavy television viewers spend an average of four and a half hours daily staring at a TV or computer screen (Dickinson, 2000).

Television viewing competes with family interaction and makes individual viewers irritable. Most people regard television as a way to relax and escape from the worries and tensions of everyday life, but studies show that sitting passively in front of a TV set, especially for long periods of time, actually puts viewers in a worse mood and makes them less able to concentrate than before they began to watch. Television desensitizes children and adults to violence and may influence children's minds more than our own educational system can. It eclipses healthy, more active pursuits.

Gaining control over the TV won't be easy; it too can be addicting. But the effort will pay off if you replace this time with activities that strengthen family ties. Family fun and traditions, begun when kids are young, weld family members together. "My favorite story about parents, kids, and TV," reports Amy Dickinson (2000, p. 81), "comes from Linda Ellerbee" the producer of children's public-affairs shows from Nickelodeon. "One night Ellerbee was trying to get the attention of her two children, who were glued to the TV. In desperation, she yanked the set out of the wall and tossed it out a second-story window. Hours later she guiltily found it lying in a heap on the lawn. She brought it inside and plugged it in. To her horror, it still worked. 'Damn!' she said. 'You can't even kill the sucker!' Not long ago," Dickinson continues,

> I realized that in my home, the TV had become like wallpaper. One of our three sets was on virtually all the time. So five weeks ago, I decided to try a modified Ellerbee—pulling the plug without tossing the set. My daughter smugly (and correctly) predicted the loss would be hardest on me. Those first few evenings without the tube seemed to last forever. But we've been reading more, playing cards, and going out for ice cream after dinner. As I write this, the kid is in the other room teaching herself to play the piano.
>
> On a recent camping trip with our TV-addicted extended family, we alone knew how to entertain ourselves. Our first night in the woods, we suggested playing charades, and it became our hilarious nightly ritual. On our last night, we held a "no-talent show," in which each person sang or told stories for the group. I don't know how long my daughter and I can hold out without TV, but we've learned some discipline and some alternatives. Maybe we can't kill the sucker—but we can control it.

ACTIVITIES FOR PARENTS AND KIDS

12.1 Ask family members to name your family traditions—daily, holidays, birthdays, and other. Which are your favorites? What new traditions would you like to establish?

12.2 One tradition worth considering is a regular date-with-a-parent night, when a busy mother or father schedules one-on-one time with just one child, participating in a favorite activity like miniature golf. In a family with more than one child, kids treasure this time because they get Mom's or Dad's full attention. (Parents and families also benefit when moms and dads schedule regular date nights for themselves!)

12.3 Foster your family's traditions and special history by having a "Family Scavenger Hunt" or starting a "Family Storybook." You can also design a family crest that depicts traditions or "trademarks" of your family.

12.4 Collect oral histories from family members. (See Appendix G.)

12.5 Play the conversational game. "Pick a Card, Any Card." (See Appendix H.)

12.6 Plan Family Fun. Ask each family member to take three note cards and on each write a fun family activity that can be done *at home*. Place the three cards in an envelope identified by the writer's name. Then, using three more cards and another envelope, write a fun family activity on each that can be done *away from home*. Once each week (or more often) take turns selecting a home-based activity from one of the envelopes. Each month (or more often) select an activity away from home. Since the latter may require funds (e.g., movies, bowling, visit to the zoo), meet as a family to develop a budget and allow each person (no matter how young) to help raise the necessary money.

REFERENCES

Dickinson, Amy. 2000. "Kick the TV Habit." *Time,* July 17, p. 81.

INTERNET SOURCES

www.loveathome.com/traditions/trd04.html
www.theantidrug.com

13 Influence Through Example and Teaching

Children who clearly understand parental expectations about abstaining from alcohol, for example, are four times less likely to drink than those who are uncertain of expectations. So as a parent, speak up! (*Drug Abuse Update,* December 1989).

Parental Example

Your own use of alcohol and other drugs will influence your children more than anything you say, more than any antidrug message they ever hear. One mother who reprimanded her son's drug experimentation had her own drug use—drinking and smoking—thrown back at her. His own drugs, the son argued, were just different from hers.

"Living your life consistent with the principles you teach is super important," a mother emphasized. If parents pretend to be paragons of virtue but don't practice what they preach, kids will see right through it. Home should be a place of truth, not deceptions. "Kids are too smart," said another parent. "If you slip off quietly and do things you wouldn't want them to do, they'll figure it out. Then they'll think it's okay for them to slip out too. You have to be a positive role model."

Research shows a generational continuity in drug use—your children are far more likely to use these substances if you do. Children of alcoholics, for example, are at higher risk of becoming alcoholic themselves. Two explanations account for this continuity: parental modeling, and emotional pathology. With *parental modeling,* teenagers imitate adults, particularly their parents. They respond to what parents model as appropriate behaviors. When alcoholic drinks and over-the-counter and prescription medications are regularly stocked in their homes, kids become familiar with them and regard their use as acceptable. "I came from a family of drinkers," an alcoholic recalled. "Some of my best drinking buddies were from my own family. I didn't have to hide my drinking from them, because I drank with them."

Parents who unwind with a drink and a cigarette after work send a message to their teenagers that drugs provide relief and relaxation and are a normal part of life. Kids typically use these "gateway" drugs before trying marijuana and other illegal substances.

When parents drink and use other substances while telling their children that they can do the same when they are "old enough," youth regard drinking and smoking as privileges of maturity. Thus they are likely to seek out the "forbidden fruit" while still in their teens. During a time when they are just beginning to learn how to deal with life's challenges, alcohol and other drugs can all too easily provide an alternative to healthy coping skills. Even if kids do not escalate to illegal drugs, their physical and emotional well-being stands at risk. Parents might want to ask themselves whether it's worth the wine rack or the six-pack.

Sidebar 13.1: A Tragic Mistake

Four teenage boys were killed on a weekend outing when the driver, who was drunk, overturned his father's car. The investigating officer asked the parents why they didn't stop their son from taking a twelve-pack of beer from the refrigerator as he left. The father sighed; the mother said, "Believe me, we've asked *ourselves* that" (Moehringer, 1996, p. 10).

Emotional pathology, the second reason for generational continuity, predisposes kids to drink and use other psychoactive drugs to deal with uncomfortable feelings. Children raised in families where substances are regularly abused often turn to drugs to cope.

The typical family profile of a drug-involved adolescent at the escalation stage is characterized by tension between kids and parents, especially when one parent—usually the father—is a heavy drinker. Typically, fathers of male alcoholics are often absent from home and, when present, serve as poor role models. Emotionally distant, they exert little effective discipline or warmth and may even treat their family cruelly.

When parents are intoxicated, children are often forced to play the caretaker role, which deprives them of healthy, playful childhood experiences. "My son became a little worry-wart when I was drinking and drugging," one such parent relates. "Our roles were reversed in some strange way and he almost became my father. But now I'm sober, a lot more confident, and have a much healthier relationship with my son."

Of these two ways in which families influence children's choices, parents' own drug use (modeling) plays an important role during the initiation stage. Emotional pathology in a family may provide a strong undercurrent at later stages of substance use. That is, children are more likely to experiment with drugs and alcohol if their parents drink, smoke, and/or rely heavily on prescription medications. They're more likely to escalate to drug *abuse* if their family life is stressful rather than supportive.

Because young people learn drinking patterns from their parents, parental abstinence from alcohol and other substances is a first line of defense against youthful initiation. "It's easier to avoid alcohol and drugs if your parents aren't into that," a teen commented.

Parental efforts to maintain quality relationships with their children and avoid the emotional problems that drug dependencies cause in the home are the best hedges against kids' escalating involvement with substances. "We have the most success with kids who have bonded with their parents and have been taught right from wrong," an adolescent-drug-treatment director observed. "We can build on that and turn them around just a little bit quicker. It also helps when their parents are drug free. To some kids, drugs are okay because their parents do it."

Parental Teaching

Setting a good example is always the best teaching method. And there are other ways to teach your children about the dangers of drugs. "We started early," a father explained,

> explaining to them the best way to live healthy and happy. Our kids all learned that drinking and smoking are not options for our family. Neither is cheating, lying, or infidelity. We've taught them that life will go better for them if they avoid these things. Old fashioned, yes, but they work. We also teach them what doesn't work, that people who get drunk usually fall short of their potential. They feel miserable and rotten, get sick and throw up, and often hurt themselves and their loved ones. Kids are smart enough to figure out that this doesn't equate with happiness and successful living.

Sidebar 13.2: Teaching Tips

Although most parents say they've talked with their children about drugs, only about one in four says his or her kids are learning a lot at home about the risks of drugs, according to a national study by the Partnership for a Drug-Free America (PDFA). Here are some tips:

- Be absolutely clear with your kids that you don't want them using drugs. Ever. Anywhere. Don't leave room for misinterpretation. And talk often about the dangers. Once or twice a year won't do it.

- Be a better listener. Ask questions and encourage kids by paraphrasing what they say to you. Ask for their input about family decisions. Your willingness to listen will encourage your children to open up to you.
- Give honest answers. Don't make up what you don't know. If asked whether you've ever taken drugs, let them know what's important: that you don't want *them* using drugs.
- Use TV reports, antidrug commercials, or school discussions about drugs to introduce the subject in a natural, unforced way.
- Don't react in a way that will cut off further discussion. If your child makes statements that challenge or shock you, turn them into a calm discussion by asking questions. Encourage kids to express their ideas.
- Role-play and practice ways to refuse drugs in different situations. Acknowledge how tough these moments can be (www. theantidrug.com).

This father had no trouble taking a stand when he caught his daughter smoking.

> I blew up but what I said wasn't half bad. I said, "Look, if you're going to rebel or whatever, at least be smart about it. Do you really want to be addicted to nicotine? It will cost you thousands of dollars, undermine your health, and cause birth defects. It's a dirty, idiotic habit. It's really dumb."

"I don't beat around the bush with my kids," said a mom.

> When it looked like my kid was using drugs, I said, "Look, someone told me they saw you using marijuana." As it turned out, it was only a rumor. So we discussed that when you're around others who use that stuff, you appear to be just like them. "If your friends are using them, leave. It's dumb! Find your own kind of fun. Be wiser and smarter."

To help prevent addiction among young people, draw a line on the abstinence side of tobacco, alcohol, and marijuana. The more kids are around these drugs, the more desensitized they become—and the more vulnerable. Take a position!

Sidebar 13.3: Mother Buying Beer for Teen

A woman buying beer for her teenage son and his friends remarked to the supermarket checker, "I figure it's better if they do it at my house where I know how much they're drinking and I have some control over it." "That's so cool," the checker replied. After she left with the beer, the next woman in line told the checker, "That's not cool at all! For her to buy that stuff for her kid and reinforce the idea that drinking is what you do at parties is just awful."

Help your children become more insightful about seductive media messages that encourage use of unhealthy products. You can do this in your home the way teachers do in media classes. "Media literacy" helps youngsters evaluate the underlying assumptions and messages in commercials, advertisements, and music. The teaching process consists of video-recording televised advertisements and dramas that glamorize alcohol and replaying them and discussing questions such as: "What is the producer telling us? How does he want us to respond? How is he trying to persuade us? How effective is the persuasion?" (See Appendix B.)

It may be useful, for example, to count the number of times that alcoholic beverages are used in a program or advertisement and analyze the messages they promote. One analysis found that alcoholic beverages are the most frequently consumed drinks in media presentations, followed by soft drinks, coffee or tea, and finally, water. In real life the order is reversed.

"We began analyzing advertisements in the print and media with our kids," a father explained.

> When they were little we talked about the motives and strategies toy manufacturers use with their ads. In ads for toy cars, they place the camera down low so the car has a tremendous size and a big sound. Kids soon figure out that manufacturers want you to buy their products so they can have your money. And they transfer this realization to other advertisements for things like liquor and cigarettes and heavy-metal music and movies. If parents give kids the tool, they can eventually figure out what is good and bad for them.

Such observations generate interesting family conversations and help make your kids less vulnerable to these powerful messages. Once young people see that alcohol messages promise popularity, friendships, romance, glamour, sophistication, adventure, and athletic prowess, a family discussion will help them understand that use of these substances actually detracts from these very qualities.

Teaching your child resistance skills can also help. With good refusal skills, youngsters can stay out of trouble and still be accepted by their peers. Identify various social situations where drugs may be offered and then role-play [act out] ways to decline without offending a well-meaning friend. Most of the time a simple "no thanks" will work. If this isn't effective the first time, kids can say it more strongly the second time. "No way!" The important point is to keep the refusal simple. The fewer the words the better. Just make sure the first word is always "no." (See Appendix I.)

Another effective response is to change the subject and talk about something else. "Try this," a friend suggests. "No thanks. By the way, do you know how the game turned out?" If pressed for a reason, some youngsters find success in saying, "Nah, I don't need them." Don't elaborate; the broken-record approach is best. If coaxed or teased by friends, a youth can leave and go do something else. "No thanks. I'm going to the movies. Want to come along?" No social offense here. If pressure builds up, just walk away.

Sidebar 13.4: Refusing Drugs Graciously

A high school student-body president gave this advice on what to do if offered alcohol or other drugs: "Never be rude about it—that really offends—and don't make an issue of it. Just say, 'I don't drink.' If your friends persist, you can add, 'I play sports,' or 'It's a religious thing.' If everything else fails, just say, 'My parents would kill me.'"

Help your kids avoid places and situations where people use alcohol and other drugs. Teach them to ask, "What's planned?" If they suspect that others will be using substances at an event, they can avoid it all together. Then help them find appealing alternative activities.

Teach your teens that when they make up their own minds and stand firm on their position, others secretly admire them. And by showing strength, they may help others think twice about using drugs. Confidence and self-direction, always admired qualities, reflect clear personal standards and goals.

Let your youngster know that in difficult times of discouragement or doubt, you will help. Be an ally, friend, and confidant, someone who is always available to listen and provide support.

Most important, encourage youths to "hang out" with friends who don't use drugs—a fundamental prevention principle. We tend to become like those with whom we spend time. Peer pressure can be positive, too. To keep themselves clean and sober, many recovering alcoholics and ex-addicts, for example, organize their lives around the concept of "righteous peer pressure." They put space between themselves and tempting friends and situations.

The following suggestions by the National Parent Teachers Association can help you and your teenagers plan drug- and alcohol-free parties. If your teen is the *host*:

- set the ground rules in advance. Specify, for example, the number of guests permitted, the off-limits areas of the house, the presence of lighting, and the ban on alcoholic drinks and other drugs;
- insist that adults walk through occasionally, mingling briefly with the guests to see that things are under control;
- help your teen have fun without chemical substances. Consider a theme party or an activity such as renting a karaoke machine or a video camera to film guests performing favorite songs;
- obey curfew and other laws, and insist on keeping the noise down so that neighbors won't be annoyed or tempted to call the police;
- consider ruling that no one who leaves the party can return, since teens sometimes leave a party to drink or use drugs and then try to come back in;
- most important, serve only nonalcoholic beverages, and allow no drugs! Be prepared to send away anyone who disobeys these rules and to call the parents of any guest causing trouble.

If your teen is a *guest:*

- know the host's name, address, and phone number;
- call the host's parents in advance to confirm that they will be at home. You may feel uncomfortable doing this, but you may be able to ease the awkwardness by asking if you can send refreshments or help in any other way;
- be sure to verify plans for any overnight stays;
- if possible, be at home while your child is at the party. If you can't do so, give your child a phone number where you can be reached, or arrange for another trusted adult to be available;
- agree with your teens that they will call home if they see trouble coming, and assure them that you will not blame them for a friend's behavior.

Good, solid parenting won't prevent your children from making mistakes, but it *will* reduce the chances that they'll make serious errors such as getting involved with mind-altering substances. Why? Because all this effort on your part spells out the most important message of all: "I care deeply about your happiness. I won't stand by watching you self-destruct."

ACTIVITIES FOR PARENTS AND KIDS

13.1 Chart your family's over-the-counter and prescription drug use for a month and then ask as a family, "Are any of our medications unnecessary?" For example, if you are taking a lot of medicine for tension headaches or indigestion, could you relieve your stress in more healthy ways or change your diet?

13.2 Ask yourself, "Is my use or non-use of tobacco, alcohol, and other drugs something I want my children to emulate? Is my behavior consistent with what I expect of them?"

13.3 Ask your family, "What have I taught you about using tobacco, alcohol, and other drugs?" How do their answers correlate with what you think you taught them?

13.4 Practice refusal skills. See Appendix I.

REFERENCES

Drug Abuse Update. 1989. December, p. 5.

Moehringer, J. R. 1996. "James Patterson Rolled His Father's Suburban and Four of His Friends Died." *Los Angeles Times Magazine,* July 28, p. 10.

INTERNET SOURCE

www.theantidrug.com

PART SIX

What Can I Do in the Community?

In addition to what you can do within your family, you can strengthen your influence against drug use through active involvement in religious, educational, and community organizations. While the government's "war on drugs" is failing miserably, your efforts in your home, neighborhood, the school, and the larger community can exert an important impact.

14 Participate with a Youth-Oriented Religious Group

People often avoid the topic of religion in conversation to minimize the risk of interpersonal conflict. Indeed, many individuals have intense feelings—favorable and unfavorable—about religion. Some had unpleasant experiences with religious zealots during childhood and felt that religion was forced on them. Others have had positive experiences and regard religion as the source of personal strength and family cohesiveness. Whatever your religious history, be aware that your family's involvement in a positive religious group can help your kids avoid drugs and alcohol.

The Benefits of Religion

Traditionally, scientists and therapists have devalued religion. "Religion has not been given much credit in the mental-health business," one psychotherapist noted. "I believe that this is one of the biggest mistakes therapists make."

Today, however, spirituality is increasingly recognized in science and clinical practice. More than thirty medical schools now offer courses on health and spirituality, and the U.S. Senate recently appropriated $50 million to set up five major centers to study mind-body medicine around the country, including the religious connection. Moreover, Harvard University now sponsors national workshops on "Spirituality and Medicine" for physicians and other health practitioners (Palevitz & Lewis, 1999).

Sidebar 14.1: Religion and Well-Being

Allen Bergin, a professor of psychology at Brigham Young University who conducts research on religion and mental health, summarized considerable evidence that religious involvement reduces "such problems as sexual permissiveness, teen pregnancy, suicide, drug abuse, alcoholism, and to some extent deviant and delinquent acts, and increases self-esteem, family cohesiveness, and general well-being. . . . Some religious influences have a modest impact, whereas another portion seem like the mental equivalent of nuclear energy.   More generally, social scientists are discovering the continuing power of religion to protect the family from the forces that would tear it down" (Raspberry, 1993, from www. heritage.org/library/categories/family).

Faith communities—organizations that help members gain spiritual insight and ethical understanding—benefit the health and welfare of participants. Six out of ten Americans regard religious faith as the most important influence in their lives, and eight out of ten say their religious beliefs provide them with both comfort and support. Many religious denominations encourage drug-free lifestyles and promote loving relationships and healthy living. They also provide positive role models for teens and their parents.

Youths from homes with a common religious belief system and shared religious activities usually choose drug-free lifestyles. Meaningful religious beliefs and enjoyable practices, consistently modeled by parents—not forced on kids—also unite families.

The relationship between religious practice and the moderate use or avoidance of alcohol is well documented, regardless of whether specific denominational beliefs prohibit the use of alcohol. The greater the religious involvement, the less likely participants are to use or abuse alcohol and other drugs (www.heritage.org/library/ then category: Family).

Those who abuse alcohol rarely have strong religious commitments. In their study of the development of alcohol abuse, David Larson and William P. Wilson, professors of psychiatry at Northwestern University School of Medicine, found that nine out of ten alcoholics had lost interest in religion in their teenage years. But for all groups they studied, religious commitment correlates with absence of drug abuse (www.heritage.org/library/).

Quitting smoking, reducing tobacco use, or avoiding it altogether is also linked with attendance at religious meetings. A study of Native Americans, for example, discovered that smokers who attended church each week used 35 percent fewer cigarettes per day than smokers who didn't attend. Among people who had taken up smoking some time in their life, those who had rarely attended church in the past year were 79 percent less likely to have quit (Spangler, Bell, & Knick et al., 1998).

Attendance at church and related religious activities has special significance for drug use among teenagers. A study of young girls ages nine to seventeen found that less than 10 percent of those who attended religious services weekly or more often indicated any drug or alcohol use, compared with 38 percent of all the girls studied (Fagan, 1996).

Shared parental attitudes toward religion are also important. If a mother and father have conflicting religious beliefs and practices, their children are more likely to use or abuse alcohol than youths from families where parents share the same religious beliefs and practices (www.heritage.org/library/categories/family).

A father remarked,

> I don't know how I could have raised my kids without religious values in our home. They live in a world of immediate self-gratification, bombarded everywhere with "get-yours-right-now" and "feel-good-quickly" messages. Without perspective, kids become spoiled and ill-prepared to deal with the reality that everyday living is not always thrilling. Unless they develop deep values, they will be poorly prepared for adulthood—paying bills, working every day.

Church participation, this same father observed, taught his children that "life is not always self-gratifying; it involves responsibility, loving, caring, and sacrificing. We need to constantly learn to do things that don't give us immediate rewards."

Religious participation offers young people the wisdom of the ages—insights from some of the world's greatest teachers and sages regarding human choices and behaviors. During the typically short-sighted and hedonistic teenage years, religion can give kids a measure of empathy and remind them of larger life issues.

Sidebar 14.2: Faith

"There are certain psychosocial conditions that add to the psyche's elasticity, and one of them has to do with the experience of not being alone in the world, the experience of essentially having support of others, including an interior experience of support, which is what faith is all about" (Lloyd Sederer, M.D., quoted in www.webmd.lycos.com).

Integrating Family and Religion

As mentioned, however, forcing religion on kids can backfire. Teens are understandably repelled when religion is imposed in a negative, harsh, or dictatorial way. Frustrated kids may respond to such pressure by going in the opposite direction to demonstrate their independence.

Successful parents use a variety of ways to make religion a positive part of their family life. "As a reminder of our spiritual roots," a Christian father said, "we hang pictures of Christ in our home." Scripture reading also benefits some families. "We raised our kids on regular scripture reading," a dad commented,

> and it brought a wholesome attitude and feeling—a spirit—into our home. It has been the most profound influence in our family. We read together each Sunday evening after dinner. Each person reads five verses. The little guys usually go play on the floor. Our children learned the stories and developed an understanding of eternal principles and appreciation of all the wondrous blessings of our lives. I can't explain it, but this has had a tremendous influence on bringing us all together.

Attending worship services, an integral activity for some families, also bonds family members. "Our family goes to church," a mother reports. "It's one of the things we do. We tell our kids, 'You are part of the family and this is something we do.'" Again, participants find that religious teachings are rarely compatible with hedonistic lifestyles, because they discourage the pursuit of short-term pleasures at the expense of long-term well-being.

Some parents may think that religious teachings, like every thing else they say to teens, "go in one ear and out the other." But keep in mind that religious participation can provide a positive peer-support group for your kids. At synagogue, mosque, or church, many young people find friendships with other teens who avoid drugs and alcohol. Selection of friends, as we saw previously, is critical in determining whether kids use substances. As drug-using peers irresistibly draw teens into drug lifestyles, clean-living friends pull in the opposite direction.

According to University of Louisville researchers Patrick H. Hardesty and Kathleen M. Kirby (1995), teens avoid choosing friends who use drugs and spurn drugs themselves—alcohol, marijuana, cocaine, crack, and amphetamines—if their families are actively religious. In this study, family religious commitment included attending religious services, praying, talking about the meaning of religious holidays, and assessing the belief that "some things are to be taken on faith." "Raising children with the practice of religion," the researchers conclude, "affords some measure of protection against illicit drug involvement during adolescence." "This is one of many studies which indicate that church attendance is a significant deterrent to delinquent behavior in adolescents," stated Dr. David B. Larson of the nonprofit National Institute for Healthcare Research (Hardesty & Kirby, 1995).

If you are willing to make religion a part of your family life, look for a religious organization that provides youth education, peer leadership, and supervised youth activities that meet adolescents' needs for adventure, independence, and peer approval. Participating in such groups not only occupies kids' time and energy, it provides "righteous peer pressure," a phrase used by heroin addicts in one treatment setting.

Under benign adult supervision, kids can plan and carry out their own religious activities. In so doing, they develop responsibility and leadership skills. As parents, be fully informed and involved in approving plans and giving appropriate support (transportation, chaperones, etc.). This involvement also provides a positive interaction between teens and parents, offering opportunities for you to praise your kids and remain actively yet nonintrusively involved in their lives.

A 15-year-old boy reported on the activities of his church youth group. Meeting each week on a school night, this group plans and carries out fun activities such as sports, canoeing and other wholesome activities. "In our youth program," he said, "we have done many service projects. We've cleaned people's yards; fed the homeless; visited rest homes; built trails, fences, and picnic benches; gathered books; and cleaned schools, beaches, roadways, and river basins. We've sent care packages and letters to missionaries, gathered food and toys for the poor and helped with the Special Olympics—just to name a few. There are opportunities to serve everywhere, every day," he added. "We should not wait for such organized projects to serve."

Sidebar 14.3: Something Worth Living and Dying For

In his book *The Pursuit of Happiness: Who Is Happy—and Why* (1992), David G. Myers notes the link between faith and emotional well-being. Religion, he observes, offers people something worth living and dying for, something bigger than themselves for which to work, a sense of connectedness, unconditional acceptance, and hope. "The peace of God, which passeth all understanding," as the Biblical apostle Paul called it, apparently offers solace and support as well as happiness (Philippians 4:7).

Beleaguered parents, overwhelmed by the demands of parenting, benefit further when religious organizations provide parent-training workshops and support groups. A network of like-minded parents can heighten parental influence in dealing with the ups and downs of adolescence. Single parents especially benefit from such networks. "It takes a village to raise a child," former First Lady Hillary Clinton reminded us. Religious communities, like villages, anchor families and make parenting easier and more successful.

ACTIVITIES FOR PARENTS AND KIDS

14.1 Ask your kids, "What matters most in life?" Discuss the idea of a life philosophy (or mission statement). Come up with a family philosophy or mission statement, then ask family members to write their personal philosophies or values, to be shared and discussed noncritically at a later family meeting.

14.2 Do you practice your religious faith with an organized group? If so, do they offer social events with like-minded people? If not, suggest that your kids identify drug-free students at school and ask them about their religious involvements. Visit several congregations to assess whether they meet your family needs. Discuss whether you want to go back.

14.3 Go on a nature walk and talk about the miracles of life all around you.

14.4 Ask each family member to write a list of at least ten things in their lives that make them happy. (Once they start writing, they may think of many more.) Share these "good things" or gratitude lists as a family. Notice how this activity affects the mood in your home. You can repeat this activity every week for four weeks.

14.5 Most religions emphasize kindness and the dignity of the individual. As a miniature community, does your family practice these values? Brainstorm ways your family can apply these values more deliberately both in daily life and in interactions with others. (For example, a father might commit to not cursing angrily at drivers who cut him off in traffic.)

REFERENCES

Fagan, Patrick. 1996. "Why Religion Matters: The Impact of Religious Practice on Social Stability." The Heritage Foundation. Backgrounder No. 1064, January 25, p. 9.

Hardesty, P. H., & Kirby, K. M. 1995. "Relation Between Family Religiousness and Drug Use Within Adolescent Peer Groups." *Journal of Social Behavior and Personality*. October 1, pp. 421–430.

Myers, David G. 1992. *The Pursuit of Happiness: Who Is Happy—and Why*. New York: W. Morrow.

Palevitz, Barry A., & Ricki Lewis. 1999. "Mixing Religion and Health: Is It Good Science?" *The Scientist*, March 29, p. 9 from: www.the-scientist.com/yr1999.

Raspberry, William. 1993. "Christmas Without Meaning? Must the Religious Make a Secret of Their Beliefs?" *The Washington Post*, December 24, p. A15 from www.heritage.org/library/categories/family.

Spangler, J. G., Bell, R. A., Knick, S., Michielutte, R., et al. 1998. "Church-Related Correlates of Tobacco Use Among Lumbee Indians in North Carolina." *Ethnicity and Disease*, 8(1), pp. 73–80.

INTERNET SOURCES

www.the-scientist.com/yr1999
www.heritage.org/libary/categories/family
www.webmd.lycos.com

15 Encourage and Support Prevention Programs at School

Schools can greatly influence your child's attitude toward drugs. Botvin's (1995) six-year study of seventh grade students, for example, found that a school-based prevention program taught by classroom teachers resulted in long-lasting reductions in tobacco, alcohol, and marijuana use. Early intervention can prevent drug use until the end of high school.

Many schools also have associated parent organizations that influence youngsters' behaviors outside school. Get involved in such programs. "How do you know what's going on at school if you're not involved?" asked one mother. "Who can you talk to when there's a problem? You need firsthand experience about what's going on."

According to a survey of nearly a thousand nine- to fourteen-year-olds conducted by the Nickelodeon channel and *Time*, there's major disagreement in many families about the extent of parental involvement in their children's education. While 92 percent of the parents in this survey said they are very interested in their kids' schoolwork, the number fell to 75 percent when the kids were asked whether this is true of their parents. Similarly, 77 percent of the parents said they help their kids with homework to help them learn more, as opposed to just checking it over to make sure it is done, but only 60 percent of the kids agreed with that. Teachers overwhelmingly said they wanted parents to be extremely involved in their kids' work, but only 3 percent of teachers said they believed parents really are. Nearly four out of ten teachers said their schools don't do enough to involve parents (Goldstein, 2000).

Sidebar 15.1: Parental Involvement at School

"I got involved with school activities," one parent explained, "when I learned my sons in junior high school were afraid to go into the restrooms because other kids were in there smoking marijuana and taunting those who didn't. They'd come home from school not having gone to the restroom all day. So I volunteered and got involved. I recommended the establishment of a parent-education program and a teacher-development program, to show teachers how to identify and help kids with drug-related problems. We got a grant from an insurance company, developed liaisons with city leaders and the County Alcohol and Drug Program, and involved these decision-makers in the lives of our kids."

School Policy

Be aware of your school's policies about alcohol and other drugs. School policies should specify what constitutes a drug offense, spell out consequences for violating the policy, describe procedures for handling violations, and build community support for the policy. No school-based prevention program will prosper without such a policy in place.

During parent-child conferences, ask how drug education is being taught. Are faculty trained to teach about alcohol and other drug use? Is drug education a regular part of the curriculum? Do children in every grade receive drug education? Is there a component for parents?

Well-designed curricula clearly specify goals, describe the purpose of each program activity and the way it works, and provide attractive, easy-to-use materials. Teacher training should prepare instructors to deal with youngsters in an encouraging and nonjudgmental way. You have a right to know about such things.

Ask to see the materials used in your school's drug-education program. Do they convey a clear message that alcohol and other drugs can be harmful? Is the information accurate and up-to-date? Does the school have referral sources for students who need extra help?

Most important, teachers and parents must treat adolescents with respect. They must understand that teenagers use drugs to assert independence, to appear mature, to gain peer acceptance, to have fun, and to cope with painful feelings.

Adolescents typically feel invulnerable and immune to the long-term health consequences of alcohol, tobacco, and other drugs. Rarely are they impressed by exaggerated claims or worries about the possibility of reduced health at midlife. Their concerns center on feeling good, looking attractive, gaining peer acceptance, performing well in school, and staying out of trouble.

Your personal involvement in appropriate school activities will strengthen the school's influence on your children's lives. In small community schools, parents personally know their children's teachers, but in large urban schools, it's harder to know individual teachers. Moreover, they exert less influence over kids. Without your participation in appropriate parent-school activities, your youngster can become anonymous and feel unimportant.

Sidebar 15.2: School Principals' Advice to Parents

- Display an interest in school activities, show enthusiasm and participate in the educational process and school activities.
- Every day when your child comes home from school, talk with him or her. Ask what he has done for the day. Get a clear picture and be supportive, not critical.
- Read to your children often and have them read to you. This gives you time together, conversation, reading practice, and language background.
- Eat dinner together at the table and not in front of the TV. Discuss the events of the day. Do more listening than talking and avoid criticism.
- Sit down with your child and establish a time schedule for study.
- Devote at least fifteen minutes of time to each child per day when you give your undivided attention—read to them, talk together, or play a game of the child's choice.
- Be firm and fair in developing family rules and in making clear the consequences of nonconformity. Don't be afraid to say "no."
- Know where your child is at all times and with whom.
- Encourage getting everything ready for school the next day and placing these materials by the door so they won't be forgotten.
- Be careful of what words and ideas you share with your children. What you say and how you say it will set the tone and goals of their lives for years to come. Use encouragement freely and criticism very seldom (Wherry, 1997, from www.par-inst.com/resources).

An exemplary program in New Zealand, called "PRYDE Parent Networks," organizes groups of parents whose children are classmates. Their objectives are to:

- provide positive group pressure that counteracts negative group pressure
- communicate openly with one another about parenting concerns
- set common guidelines for their children's behavior and agree to provide appropriate consequences for unacceptable actions
- help their children plan activities that follow these guidelines

- educate themselves about adolescent drug and alcohol use
- function as a continuing, adaptable parent-support group
- use the telephone to establish an even wider parent-support network.

Each group discusses and decides its own guidelines for kids' activities outside the home (especially during evening hours) and for hosting and attending parties (Boswell, 1998).

Classroom Drug Education

Unfortunately, research shows that traditional classroom-based drug education with children is generally ineffective. The information approach (teaching youngsters the physiological consequences of drug use) assumes that once youngsters understand how drugs harm their bodies they will "just say no"! Although some do—one father said, "I asked my son about drugs and he answered, 'I have no intention of taking drugs and ruining my health'"—drug information stimulates the curiosity of other children, creating interest where none existed before. Moreover, the "scare-tactics" method may unwittingly undermine teacher credibility and challenge adolescents to prove their daring by trying drugs.

Kids are usually intrigued by the various drug paraphernalia police officers display when they come to class. Also, recovering drug addicts invited to proclaim the evils of drugs inadvertently glamorize their use and convey the idea that addiction is not a big deal: "Just look at me; I'm a cool guy who has lived an exciting life, and now I'm here as a role model."

The most effective school programs help students identify drug-use situations and then teach specific resistance skills that lead to positive social outcomes. They help students identify the source of drug-use pressures (both external and internal), and then let youths practice techniques to resist these pressures. But when interpersonal skills are taught with no mention of their relationship to alcohol and other drugs, youngsters fail to make the necessary connection. Students resist drugs when they learn that doing so will bring positive social results.

Ideally, drug education begins during the first three or four years of school. During this time, the curriculum focuses on general nutrition and ways to keep one's body healthy. Building on this foundation, kids in grades four and five can learn the assertiveness and communication skills that build their self-esteem.

This lays a base for teaching resistance skills during grades six to eight, focused on adolescents' primary concerns—how to be popular and have positive peer relationships. At this stage, youngsters need to learn how to recognize the social pressures to use party drugs, and to develop the motivation and resistance skills necessary to walk away. If youngsters can avoid drug entanglement during this time without losing social status, it is highly unlikely that they will get caught in the net of drug involvement.

Although the potential for effective prevention programs declines during the high school years, kids at this stage can still learn personal responsibility regarding drug-related issues such as drinking and driving. Formal, clear, and consistent school rules about substance use on campus are essential.

Resistance skills and motivation are most effective when respected, drug-free peers get involved in the teaching process. Adolescents are much more likely to respond favorably to information from other youths who understand their concerns. When high-status youth leaders promote the view that drug use is "uncool," they generate positive peer pressure.

Not all antidrug-education programs work. Lecturing is the least effective approach; active involvement and repeated practice, such as role-playing, are much more effective. Small-group discussion and written exercises are equally crucial. Brainstorming and the opportunity to act out successful solutions to high-pressure situations help kids develop a variety of techniques for refusing drugs when offers actually come up.

Sidebar 15.3: Encouraging Homework

- Organize a regular place for homework, a desk or table in a quiet room away from TV and other distractions and where there's plenty of light.
- Encourage your child to budget his time and to routinely follow a schedule for homework.
- You may want to implement a rule, "No TV until homework is finished." This will be the most effective if no one else watches TV during this time.
- Do the most difficult and required homework assignments first and save the easier subjects for later; finish the optional assignments last, even if they're more fun.
- Encourage your child to talk about how much she's accomplished and learned; listen, discuss, and praise (*Parents Make the Difference! Newsletter.* 2000. From www.par-inst.com/resources/44).

Extracurricular Events

Get involved in extracurricular events. Organize with other parents and meet with school officials to provide drug-free socials. Every year, parents in one California high school, for example, organize an all-night celebration for graduating seniors, providing a safe, drug-free environment. The location is kept a secret until that night so students cannot devise plans to include alcohol and other drugs in the celebration.

On the night of graduation, students are shuttled to the undisclosed location where they can participate in a wide variety of activities, such as playing casino games, dancing, competing in contests, and wall-climbing. "It's always literally off-the-wall stuff that does appeal to kids," said the high school principal. "Parents came up with the idea to host Grad-Night after they saw similar programs in other school districts, and, fortunately, not because of a graduation-night tragedy involving drinking and driving (Gottlieb, 1999).

Sidebar 15.4: Party Agreement

Parents concerned about their teenagers' attending parties where alcohol is served or that lack adult supervision usually have to depend on the trust they place in their children. Sponsored by the local ministerial association, parents in one community were invited to sign the following Parent Pledge. Those who did received a directory of the names of other parents who also signed.

The pledge states: "I take the responsibility to ensure that all social events in my home involving teenagers will be chaperoned and free from alcohol, tobacco, and other drugs. I will also provide information to parents or guardians who request confirmation of social arrangements involving their children."

About 650 parents in this community have signed these pledges, sent over the past two spring semesters in cooperation with the county school district to about nine thousand homes (Needham, 2000, p. B1).

If these kinds of things aren't happening in your kids' schools, get involved.

ACTIVITIES FOR PARENTS AND KIDS

15.1 Ask your kids about the interpersonal climate at school. Do they feel safe? Is drug and alcohol use generally restricted to certain areas, or does it occur throughout the school? What can they, and you, do to improve the situation? As a family, brainstorm a list of ideas.

15.2 With your kids' help, find out what antidrug programs are in place at their school(s). Do these programs include role-playing and other active participation? Are peer role models involved? Or do the programs feature just lecturing and scare tactics? How often are the programs implemented? If they are unsatisfactory, discuss how you as a family can help effect change. Which of your friends and neighbors would be interested in helping out? What drug- and alcohol-abstaining teen leaders might be willing to serve as peer role models? What steps will you take?

REFERENCES

Boswell, Vesta. PRYDE in New Zealand (pamphlet), National Resource Centre, Oxford Street, P.O. Box 32, Lyttelton, N.Z. (E-mail: pryde@ihng.co.nz).

Botvin, Gilbert J., Schinke, S., & Orlandi, M. A. 1995. "School-Based Health Promotion: Substance Abuse and Sexual Behavior." *Applied & Preventive Psychology.* Summer, 4(3), pp. 167–184.

Goldstein, Andrew. 2000. "Paging All Parents: A Survey Shows Many Moms and Dads Are Not as Involved with Their Kids as They Think They Are." *Time*, 156(1), July 3, p. 47.

Gottlieb, Michael. 1999. "Agoura Keeps Grad Night Secret." *Los Angeles Times.* ("Our Times" Supplement), February 10, p. 2.

Needham, Nancy K. 2000. "Parents Take Pledge: No Teen Drinking." *Los Angeles Times.* September 2, pp. B1, B9.

Parents Make the Difference! 2000. From: www.par-inst.com/resources.

Wherry, John. 1997. "What Principals Would Tell Parents to Help Parents Help Their Children." From: www.par-inst.com/resources.

16 Encourage Community Service

Helping others gives us a warm feeling called a "helper's high." Teens who attend weekend youth conferences that include many enjoyable activities—dances, dinners, stimulating self-improvement workshops, sleep-overs, and service projects (such as chaperoning developmentally disabled contestants at the Special Olympics or painting an elderly widow's home) enjoy the service activities most. *Giving* rather than *getting* typically tops the list of things they enjoy most and remember longest. Unlike psychoactive drugs, which provide only substitute highs, altruistic service yields the real thing.

Regular service does wonders for a family. When a group of eight-year-old boys were offered candy, one of them carefully picked out a red piece, then commented that he was going to give it to his younger brother since that was his favorite flavor. Their parents cultivated this loving bond by encouraging family members to serve one another. At a weekly family meeting, each person secretly draws the name of another family member from a jar, and during the week does something to help them. Then at the next meeting they discuss their experiences.

Sidebar 16.1: Do Good, Feel Good

"I really looked forward to going to the Senior Care Center each week," said a teenage girl, "not just because of the good I was doing there, but because of how good it made me feel about myself. It's hard to be sad when you're doing service!" (Zone, 2000).

Kids involved in family and community service not only tend to stay out of trouble, they become better people. And families who serve together grow closer as they help improve their community. "The skills I've developed as a result of my community work have really helped me be a better parent," said a single mother of four. "My kids have followed my example and have become involved in youth-leadership activities."

Fortunately, a lot of Americans have already discovered the rewards of service. Approximately one hundred million individuals, or about one out of every two people over the age of thirteen, have decided to get involved in community programs that support family well-being (Ribeau, 1999). Strong families offer the greatest potential for preventing youth drug use. Community service strengthens your family as well as the families you serve, for a positive "double whammy."

Recognizing this, savvy parents plan service activities for the entire family. "Our expedition to Peru was an investment in the growth and development of our family," said such a parent. "We wanted to help those of a different culture and economic base and in return, we hoped that they would help us appreciate our world more. Our expectations were realized and the returns many" (Ashton, 1999, p. 3). "I cannot believe the change in my thinking. I was only there for a short time, but I love the people and I love what I could do for them and for me" (*CHOICE*, 1996).

American kids who grow up with every convenience are surprised to witness how little others have. "I learned that clean water, clean food, and a clean place to sleep are luxuries," one said. A 14-year-old, who formerly compared his material possessions with those of his peers, exclaimed, "Wow, we have a floor in our house." . . . "We live in a palace compared to others in the world" (Hemming, 1999, p. 5).

One family saved the money they would ordinarily spend on Christmas gifts to help an impoverished Third-World village (see the *CHOICE Humanitarian* described in Activity 16.2). "We didn't buy any gifts for the family," a parent commented. "The trip was our gift to each other. When Christmas morning came I thought the kids would be disappointed. They weren't, and in fact we went on another family Christmas expedition to Vietnam" (Hemming, 2000, pp. 4–5). "Watching tears well up in people's eyes as they see water piped into their homes and schools for the first time," said one youth, "is one of the most fulfilling moments I have had" (McMullin and Sorensen, 2000, p. 5).

Organizing Service Groups

You don't have to go far to serve. Start your own family- or neighborhood-service organizations. For example, one mother of six started a nonprofit neighborhood organization to provide service opportunities for children ages two to thirteen called *Kids Who Care*. The members of the group feel that the benefits of participating far outweigh the small amount of time it takes—usually less than an hour each month.

The dozen or so members meet once a month, alternating houses. Participation requires little preparation, for the group adheres to the same yearly schedule:

- October: Mental Health Awareness Month. Contribute used items for a local mental-health thrift store and large-size clothing items for the homeless.
- November: Fund-raiser for the rescue mission's Thanksgiving dinner. The kids pool their own money to provide for the homeless.
- December: Contribute and deliver new toys and canned food to the Salvation Army for needy children.
- January: Contribute used Christmas cards for children's art fund-raiser.
- February: Make valentines for nursing-home residents.
- March: Contribute used and/or new books to a local home for abused children or the hospital.
- April: Earth Day activity. Snip six-pack plastic rings, plant a tree or bulbs in the neighborhood.

These activities, all geared to younger children, can be adapted to any locale. A mother reported that *Kids Who Care* has simplified her family life because it changed her kids' focus from "What am I going to get?" to "What can I do for someone else?" Her kids are less materialistic now, she reports, for they've had an opportunity to see that many others have less than they do.

A small-scale, low-maintenance, grassroots organization like this can provide another benefit as well: the opportunity for neighborhood families to get to know one another. This familiarity creates a close-knit support system for busy parents (St. James, 1998).

Sidebar 16.2: Matt's Service

One father described his son's community service: "A man in our neighborhood who is disabled with multiple sclerosis came up with a project that helped my son and benefited a lot of other kids. He fixes up abandoned bikes and gives them to the disadvantaged. My thirteen-year-old son and two of his friends go over after school to help him for a couple of hours. In less than a year they've collected hundreds of old bikes, fixed them up, and given them to charities and churches for distribution. The entire project is computerized; my son has learned how to track a repair job from start to finish! He just loves being so involved and can't wait to get there each day. It's a terrific example of what one person can do to make a big difference for a lot of needy people. 'I like the hands-on work, and it makes me feel good to help other people and give them some kind of transportation,' said Matt. 'Once we even got some thank-you cards from some kids who got our bikes—that was *real* cool.'"

Families Fighting Back

You may also want to consider organizing other families to fight against drug abuse. Take a look at what these families did:

- *Santa Fe, New Mexico.* It's amazing what kid power—and a little peanut butter and jelly—can accomplish! Last year, 350 students packed the New Mexico state capitol to talk to their lawmakers about passing a mandate that would make it illegal to sell tobacco to kids under eighteen. They brought the lawmakers peanut butter and jelly sandwiches to lunch on! A month later, the law passed.
- *Marmath, North Dakota.* What can just two kids do? Plenty, it turns out, when the two are Justin Fischer and Eric Sonsalla! The only students in their grade (the whole school has just thirty-two students), they wanted to make their school smoke-free. Eric, age eleven, admits he was "pretty nervous" when they shared this idea with the school board. But the board agreed that smoking stinks—and now nobody can smoke at Marmath Public School. "It was a really fun experience," Eric says.
- *Belvidere, Illinois.* Students at the Perry Elementary School think magazines read by kids should not print tobacco ads. So they picked some magazines—including *Sports Illustrated* and *Hot Rod*—from the school library and wrote letters to the editors, asking them to stop running these ads. When the editors didn't write back, the library canceled the subscriptions.
- *Perth Amboy, New Jersey.* "Sometimes adults think kids don't know what they're talking about," says George Vega, seventeen. But George can tell grown-ups a thing or two about tobacco advertising—and he did! His group, HORA (Hispanics on the Rise Again), surveyed cigarette billboards in his hometown. They found there were more signs in Hispanic neighborhoods than anyplace else. "They put billboards by churches and schools and in parks where kids play," he complains. HORA is talking to the city council about dumping the signs. "We want to remove tobacco billboards," says George, "and replace them with ones for milk or vegetables—something healthy and positive for kids."

- *Boston, Massachusetts.* "Read my lips—don't smoke!" With TV and newspaper reporters looking on, Sean Donahue heard his voice ring out across the lawn of the Massachusetts statehouse. More than a hundred kids—waving banners and signs that read "FRESH AIR" and "SMOKING STINKS —let out a giant roar. "It was exciting," says Sean, remembering his first antismoking rally. But Sean did more than just talk. After his rousing speech, he led a parade of wagons to the state capitol. The wagons were filled with petitions asking the Secretary of State to raise the state tobacco tax by twenty-five cents. (According to the Surgeon General, cigarette taxes save lives because high prices make some people stop smoking.) The hard work gathering those petitions paid off: Massachusetts voters approved the law raising the tax (www.cdc.gov/tobacco/sgr4kids/coast.htm).

Neighborhoods Fighting Back, an organization of residents in South Central Los Angeles, effectively fought the licensing of crime-magnet liquor stores, quick-trick motels, and "cans-for-drugs recycling centers" in their neighborhoods. Fed up with unresponsive city officials, they held regular community meetings, established an 800-number hotline to track complaints, and picketed and marched, forcing the city to become accountable for enforcing the law in these nuisance centers. One offending liquor store was nicknamed "Bucket of Blood" because the store's lot was often the site of muggings and other atrocities. When this store was forced out of business, a resident exclaimed, "People used to run the traffic light at this corner just to avoid getting mugged or harassed by the drug dealers. I can't believe how quiet it is now!" (*The Movement*, 1998).

Consider a "culture jamming" project. The advertising industry filches American's most cherished images, language, and values. Culture jammers use the same tactics to counter their adversaries' ideology. They meet the enemy on its own turf—taking space on billboards, in magazine-ad slots, and on commercial television. They even distribute t-shirts—to send critical messages in the style of the targeted offenders.

Some examples:

- A magazine ad features a riderless horse in a cemetery, with the caption "Marlboro Country."
- A billboard ad shows a bedraggled woman sitting at a breakfast table with a glass of vodka in her hand. The caption: "Every morning's a Smirnoff morning."
- A television commercial shows an innocent-looking youngster with a fixed stare, as the voice-over announces: "Kathy is eight, and she's addicted. It changes the way she talks, the way she acts, the way she thinks. She's addicted to television."

- A t-shirt boasts a familiar-looking camel. While puffing away, the camel holds a name-brand packet of cigarettes in one hand and a sickle in the other. The caption: "Smooth reaper." This ad, the jammers boast, is a "dead ringer" for the original.

The culture-jam movement's objective is to disperse the cloud of commercialism and the acid-rain-of-the-mind that television pours down on us. As Professor Stuart Ewens of Hunter College explained, culture jammers hope to create another kind of world in which people understand that commodities should be in the service of human beings, rather than human beings devalued "in favor of the commodity."

Adds Kalle Lasn, a ringleader of the Canadian culture-jam movement and editor of *Adbusters Magazine*, "We vow to regain custody of our minds, and thereafter to resist the muck of commercialism" (Collins, 1992, p. M5).

Sidebar 16.3: Activists Target Importer of Bidis

"School children, antitobacco activists, and a county supervisor called Monday on a local firm to stop importing sweetly flavored cigarettes they claim are more dangerous than domestic brands and target youths. The twenty-five protesters presented petitions they said had a thousand signatures to Kretek International, one of the nation's biggest importers of Bidis, or Beadies, which come in such flavors as strawberry, chocolate, and cherry.

Wearing red shirts and jackets, the antitobacco activists carried placards and marched a few blocks to Kretek's headquarters. 'It's a shame to spend all that money getting rid of Joe Camel and we end up with chocolate-flavored cigarettes,' a leader said" (O'Donoghue, 2000).

Family efforts can make a difference. For example, some parents effectively lobby government leaders to reduce youth drug use in the following ways:

- Restrict the number of retail alcoholic-beverage outlets and the hours they operate.
- Raise taxes on alcoholic beverages.
- Prohibit the marketing of alcoholic beverages to underage drinkers.
- Prohibit commercials, billboards, and other advertising messages implying that success goes along with the use of chemical substances.
- Keep signs advertising alcohol and tobacco away from schools.

Call your County Coordinator of Alcohol and Drug Programs and ask how you can get involved. Or, depending on your time, energy, and other resources, consider one of these options:

- *The mass media.* Let television network executives know how you feel about commercials and programming that normalize alcohol, tobacco, and other drug use.
- *Advertising agencies.* Lobby advertising executives to develop self-regulating policies that discourage marketing messages that directly or indirectly glamorize the use of alcohol, tobacco, and other harmful substances, especially to children.
- *Religious and voluntary organizations.* Establish community-based prevention councils to promote and coordinate innovative programs. Sponsor parent-training sessions and parent-support groups. A Catholic priest in Chicago, for example, waged a minicampaign against the placement of billboard ads for alcohol and/or tobacco in low-income minority urban areas. "When you target a particular race of people with [ads for] two of the nation's top killers, that's genocide," he charged (Secter, 1990).
- *Health-care providers.* Encourage state boards that license physicians, nurses, psychologists, social workers, and family counselors to require adequate training in drug-prevention strategies and recognition of drug dependence. Push for health-warning labels on all containers and advertisements for alcoholic beverages.
- *Schools.* Encourage adoption of a policy that requires high school students to complete a sequence of drug-education courses. Establish credential-renewal policies requiring teachers to demonstrate competence in drug- and alcohol-prevention strategies. Initiate and support peer-leadership training programs and counseling services to develop and reinforce positive peer pressure.
- *Private sector and public employees.* Sponsor workplace health-promotion programs that benefit families. Help employers understand that when things go well for employees at home, things also go better at work.

For additional ideas, see my book (with D. Ziedonis), Handbook on Drug Abuse Prevention (1995).

Clearly, parents who organize and work together can exert a significant impact. "If I were to give any advice to parents," a community activist advises, "it's to get involved and make a difference. Pitch in to make things better for our families and kids."

ACTIVITIES FOR PARENTS AND KIDS

16.1 As a family, research the service opportunities in your area. Churches, convalescent homes, and shelters are good places to start, and local government officials can often provide information. Set practical goals for your family's involvement, and schedule your participation in advance. Some cities have clearinghouses for a variety of service projects. For example, L.A. Works offers individuals and families in Los Angeles a full calendar of project possibilities.

16.2 Contact CHOICE Humanitarian, a nonprofit, nondenominational organization comprised of volunteers committed to helping indigenous peoples in developing nations. CHOICE expeditions, unique and adventurous, provide experiences to be treasured for a lifetime. You pay your own way (most expenses are tax deductible). You might work on building a much needed school, health post, greenhouse, well, pump, or cistern. You may also teach literacy, healthcare, or agriculture, or help on other small-scale enterprises. CHOICE offers manpower, materials, appropriate technology, and education for expeditions that generally run 10–20 days. You work side-by-side with villagers on specific projects. CHOICE also provides training materials and briefing workshops; organizes your travel and accommodations; prepares the village for your arrival; and facilitates your efforts while on site. "I would encourage anyone who desires adventure, along with the chance to serve and aid others, to join CHOICE in a future expedition. You will not only be changing and enriching the lives of others, but your own life as well" (Chambers, 1997). Contact CHOICE at 1937 South 300 West, Salt Lake City, UT 84115. 801-474-1937, fax 801-474-1919, e-mail: info@choice.humanitarian.org, www.ok.com/choice.

REFERENCES

Ashton, Crystal. 1999. "Upcoming Expeditions." *Perspective.* A newsletter of CHOICE Humanitarian, Fall/Winter, pp. 2–3.

Chambers, Erin. 1997. "Learning About Ourselves, Helping Others." Lake Oswego, *Oregon Review,* August 7.

CHOICE. A publication of Humanitarian Projects and Expeditions, 1996. Spring.

Collins, Ronald K. 1992. "Waging War on Cultural Pollution." *Los Angeles Times,* November 22, p. M5.

Coombs, Robert H., & Douglas Ziedonis. 1995. *Handbook on Drug Abuse Prevention: A Comprehensive Strategy for the Abuse of Alcohol and Other Drugs.* Boston: Allyn & Bacon.

Hemming, Jan. 1999. "Going to the Mountain to Give." *Perspective.* A newsletter of CHOICE Humanitarian, Fall/Winter, pp. 4–5.

McMullin, D., & Sorensen, R. 2000. "Bolivia, Mi Escualita Project." *Perspective.* A newsletter of CHOICE Humanitarian, Spring/Summer, p. 5.

O'Donoghue, Paul. 2000. *Daily News,* February 1, p. 1.

Ribeau, Sidney A. 1999. "Afterword," in *Serving Children and Families through Community–University Partnerships: Success Stories.* T. R. Chibucos and R. M. Lerner, Eds. Boston: Kluwer Academic Publishers.

Secter, Bob. 1990. "Priest Pleads Moral Right to Deface Ads: Chicagoan Says Heavy Use of Outdoor Liquor, Tobacco Signs in Poor Areas Is Genocide." (Michael Pfleger). *Los Angeles Times,* August 16, A5.

St. James, Elaine. 1998. "These Children Help Raise Their Village." *Los Angeles Times*, April 13, p. S7.

The Movement. 1998. Bilingual Newsletter of the Community Coalition for Substance Abuse Prevention and Treatment, Spring.

Zone, Judy. 2000. "The Helping Locally to Help Globally Program," *Perspective*. A newsletter of CHOICE Humanitarian, Fall/Winter, p. 9.

I N T E R N E T   S O U R C E S

www.cdc.gov/tobacco
www.family.go.com
www.ncadd.org/news40.html
www.ok.com/choice

PART SEVEN

Where Can I Get Help?

Parenting techniques discussed in earlier chapters are particularly effective, of course, if implemented consistently when your children are in their early years. A strong bond of affection and goodwill will ease you through the turbulent years of adolescence.

If, however, you are getting a late start, or your adolescent is out of control, seek professional help—and don't be too hard on yourself. No child-rearing technique is foolproof, and some children are just much harder to raise than others. You may have done everything correctly yet still face major problems. Reach out for help. And, to quote Winston Churchill, "Never, never, never give up!"

You may need to find a family therapist, a licensed professional with a good track record in helping clients with substance-abuse problems. Ask around; talk to others you trust who are knowledgeable. Ask experts at the local university, your family doctor, or your pediatrician to point you in the direction of the best qualified help. Once you compile a list of helping professionals, ask for references and check on their "track record." Past performance is the best predictor of how effective they will be with your youngster and family.

To find a good program, call your local Council on Alcoholism and Drug Dependence. Look in the Yellow Pages of your phone book under "Alcohol and Drugs" or contact the National Council on Alcoholism and Drug Dependence (12 West 21st Street, 7th floor, New York, NY 10010; 212-206-6770), which has 150 affiliate councils across the country, each responding uniquely to the community it serves. A council in central California, for example, directs all the publicly funded treatment programs of that county. These councils provide information, assessment, referral, and support to individuals and their families in need of treatment and recovery services. "None of us tries to operate a competitive business," reports one council director.

> We aren't looking for market share. Our role is to inform the public and to provide direct services or refer them to agencies who can best meet their specific needs. In our case, we offer outpatient and education services geared to adolescents, young adults, and their families.

A treatment specialist agrees:

> The councils are the best libraries for what's available in the community. They're the ones who normally have their fingers on the pulse about the available resources. There are lots of different hotlines, but most are financed by hospitals, or outpatient programs that try to channel the caller to themselves. All in all, the council is the best place to call. (See Appendix J for other organizations and helplines.)

Unfortunately, services for American youngsters and their families greatly diminished in the 1990s. "The revolution in health services—managed care—has mostly killed off adolescent treatment for chemical dependence and psychiatric care nationwide," a council director laments.

> So, we try to fill the gap of what's missing in the community. At no charge, we provide kids and their families with information and access to all the relevant programs, both for kids and for the parent. We put all that information together for them. All councils are objective sources of information. We are the best first call that a parent can make.

Some programs that will likely prove helpful to you are parent-training workshops, parent-support groups, family therapy, residential drug treatment, and twelve-step programs. They will be only partially effective, however, if they don't involve the entire family. One reality should be clear: We're all in this together.

CHAPTER

17 Parent-Training Workshops

Parent-training workshops can help you regain control of both your emotions and your home. "I've seen some wonderful results in parent training," an educator reports. "When parents learn how to manage their own emotions and to treat their kids with kindness and firmness, they experience improvements at home and their kids do better at school."

These classroom sessions will strengthen your skills, build your confidence, and give you perspective on parenting. You will learn how to reverse the downward spiral at home. "I teach parents how to build loving bonds with their kids," an effective parent trainer reports. Feeling protected and cared for is vital to every child's well-being. "If parents hit and shout, kids withdraw and become resentful and see the parent as a source of danger and pain. They feel betrayed and abandoned. If home isn't a safe haven, what's a child to do?"

The Benefits of Parent Training

Sidebar 17.1: Language of the Heart

Never underestimate the power of politeness. Just by speaking courteously, you may be able to bring out the best in the people you live with. Give them a chance to talk. Listen patiently. And soften your voice. A soft voice can tame adult anger and smooth over teenage traumas. As for little children—they love whispers. Stooping down to their level and looking directly into their eyes can make the difference between heartaches and heart songs.

Heartaches	*Heart Songs*
"You didn't stay inside the line."	"That's special. I can see that you worked hard."
"Look how dirty you are!"	"Looks like you had fun today."
"What's that supposed to be?"	"I like black."

"NO!"	"Let's talk about that before we decide."
"Get over here right now!"	"I need you with me."
"I TOLD YOU SO."	"That was harder than you thought."

(Jasinek & Ryan, 1988)

Parent-training workshops are designed to help you feel better about yourself and your children and communicate more positively and effectively with those at home. You will learn to identify appropriate and inappropriate behaviors, to reinforce the former and discourage the latter, and to shift the focus of parent-child interactions from generally negative to specifically positive.

A former U.S. Attorney General advocated parent skill-building as a key factor in deterring drug abuse and crime. But parent training isn't just for dysfunctional families, or for those whose kids are causing big problems. "*All* families benefit from parent training," emphasized a parent educator. "No one is exempt from needing parenting skills that build happy and healthy kids. I uncritically accept all parents into my groups and assume they're doing the best they can—and we move from there. There should never be a stigma!"

Attending workshops shows that you are willing to learn and grow and that you care. Seeking outside help means you are a survivor, not a failure. "Few of us have had any training at all except the example set by our own parents," observed an instructor.

> And, unfortunately, we are prone to perpetuate their same, often negative patterns and repeat the same mistakes. I help parents go back into their own childhood to review the things they did or had done to them—things they didn't like. After they realize that they're repeating history, I help develop the tools they'll need to change.

"I've taught hundreds of parenting classes over the years," observed an educator,

> and if I could sum it all up I'd say that parents have a very, very difficult time learning how to listen. No matter how many hours they've spent in therapy, ninety-nine percent go home and make the same mistakes: winning arguments, dictating commands and being authoritarian. Overcoming that tendency is the biggest problem parents face today. It's just not in our nature, it seems, to sit down and listen.

Studies show that parenting skill-building programs greatly improve parents' attitudes and behaviors, which in turn positively influences their children. When Frederic Medway analyzed twenty-seven studies evaluating parent-training programs, he found that parents who participated in these programs experienced 62 percent more positive gains than comparison groups who did not participate. Equally strong gains were found among their children. "Whatever knowledge, skill, and change in parenting philosophy is communicated to these parents," he concluded, "it is directly carried over to their children" (Morrow, 1994, p. 3).

Everyone benefits from parent training. The Los Angeles Department of Water and Power sponsors parenting classes and reports that they save $2.50 for every $1.00 invested in their work-family programs. And participants develop greater empathy, understanding, and acceptance of their kids—who in turn become healthier and more socially responsible and do better in school (*Los Angeles Times*, 1996).

Sidebar 17.2: Parent Project

Parent Project, a national parent-training program begun in 1988 by retired police sergeant Ralph Fry in Pomona, California, seeks to reintegrate out-of-control youth back into society. A series of classes has helped parents—about fifteen thousand at last count—to better understand their kids and curb inappropriate behaviors. Parents attend six three-hour meetings where they are introduced to the world in which children and teens make difficult decisions about alcohol, drugs, sex, and violence. After the presentations, participants break into smaller groups and discuss homework assignments (for example, compiling a list of phone numbers and addresses of their children's friends). The goal is to help overworked parents "get into the minds of their kids and let them know they're loved even as they discipline them." "It's a scary world out there today," said Fry, "not at all like the world in which our generation grew up. But many parents still aren't aware of how much that world has changed" (Hanna, 1996, p. E3).

Parent-training programs also make good use of new technologies. The Office of National Drug Control Policy offers profiles of fourteen well-known parent-education programs, including brief descriptions of contents, evaluation information, and program contracts. The programs target various age and ethnic groups and a range of family problems, but most have some focus on substance-abuse prevention. The resource guide also has a list of Internet sites on parenting education. The list encompasses federal agencies and clearinghouses, foundations, advocacy organizations, networks, and other types of organizations. (To obtain this information, check out this Web site: www.whitehousedrugpolicy.gov/prevent/parenting/r_foreword.html).

Workshop Formats and Techniques

Whatever program you select, avoid courses that rely solely on lectures. A workshop format where you can rehearse newly acquired skills is essential. Ideally, parents from several families meet with a group leader to discuss and rehearse ways of working out common child-management problems. It's not easy, especially at first, to overcome your initial shyness, and to admit your problem, but practicing in front of a group will be worthwhile. The best learning is experiential and active; the worst involves passive listening.

Workshop sessions may also indirectly help you resolve any outstanding marital problems. When recurring conflicts—often centering on differences related to child-rearing approaches—cause turmoil between spouses, your influence weakens and the risk increases that kids will withdraw and become susceptible to outside influences. "Because some parents have a lot of trouble communicating between themselves," a workshop leader observed,

> their kids get conflicting messages and easily manipulate parents. I help them get their act together so they can present a united position. It was really interesting that when a divorcing couple took our course, not only did their son respond to their new discipline system, they started talking to each other using "I messages." I don't know if they got back together, but at least they were communicating with each other.

Workshop sessions usually start with reminders of what it's like to be an adolescent. Recalling how you were either criticized and punished or praised and rewarded by your parents helps you identify with and understand your youngsters better. Parents usually treat their children similarly to how they were treated by *their* parents. "A lot of parents are very authoritarian," a trainer observed,

> so I use a lot of role-playing to help them realize how it makes kids feel. Parents play the role of teenager and I play the parent. I'll go out in the hall and shout, "Turn off that TV and get down here for dinner!" We'll discuss how they feel after hearing this and then compare an approach that gives their kid some dignity. "We're going to eat in five minutes. Could you start getting ready?"

Parents learn to avoid an overall negative assessment of their child by describing a specific adolescent behavior that they want to change. Typically, these specific behaviors center on drug experimentation, selection of friends, school performance, household chores, curfew violation, lying, and disrespectful attitudes and language toward parents and other adults.

You will discover techniques to encourage the desirable behaviors while decreasing the objectionable ones. These techniques include praise, limit-setting, and mild social punishment such as (temporarily) ignoring. You will develop skills to manage conflict, to express anger constructively, and to reduce destructive emotional outbursts. You'll also learn to communicate expectations directly, to consistently follow through, and to negotiate family contracts for mediating disputes. These contracts, mutually agreed on by all participating family members, will help you negotiate workable solutions to difficult problems. Involving your teen in the contracting process is critical. Expression of free will is essential for all, and especially vital for a developing adolescent.

Effective behavior contracts include these features:

- They request a positive change. For example, a youngster might want to include a provision that asks parents to speak in a soft voice (not yell) when they ask the youngster to do something.
- They make specific requests. Rather than saying, for example, "You need to get home on time," an effective contract will stipulate, "I would like you home by 5:30 p.m. for dinner."
- They divide requested behavior into small steps toward the desired goal, rather than describe a huge, unreachable leap.
- They include encouragement for every act of compliance. The contract should indicate that if your children fulfill some part of the agreement, you will offer a token reward. Ask them what they would like.

Because kids often break contracts, you'll need to make frequent revisions. As you learn more about the problem and refine your technique, the contract will improve. If the desired behavioral change is either too hard or too easy, update your contract. If it works, stick with it another week and check again. Did you give incentives and encouragement? If not, what interfered, and what can you do to revise the contract?

Youths are expected to comply with several hundred rules each day at school and home with little, if any, input in defining these rules. Kids allowed to present their point of view and to help develop solutions are more likely to comply, and to do so with a much better attitude.

In parent-training workshops, you will also learn to use good listening skills, to express negative feelings appropriately, to make specific and positive requests of your children, and to encourage homework and school success. In short, you will learn how to avoid becoming a negative force in your family. You will find out how to develop and state a clear family position regarding the use of alcohol and other drugs.

The basic format for effective parent-training sessions usually includes the following:

- A review of the homework assignment from the prior session, and an assessment of what you have learned, how well it worked, and how you might further improve your newly acquired skills;
- A brief explanation by the workshop leader of the new skill being presented during that session, the rationale for the new technique, and the situations where it will most likely be effective;
- Modeling of the new skill, with the trainer playing the role of parent and a class member taking the role of adolescent;
- Each parent's explaining their understanding of this new principle and practicing the new skill with the guidance of the leader;
- A homework assignment to apply the new skill to your home situation.

As mentioned, you will report on the success of your homework at the next session. "I try to build up each parent's self-esteem," a trainer commented.

Some of them have gone through divorce and have other devastating problems, so I try to build them up. On homework assignments, I only write positive things. I also ask parents to indicate on a questionnaire all the good things about themselves and to share with the group something they like about themselves. Sometimes it's the only praise they've gotten in a long time and it makes them feel good. When they start being positive about themselves, it is easier for them to see things they like in their kids.

Sidebar 17.3: Self-Quiz

What do you do?

1. Your child comes home from school and tells you that a boy hit him.
   1. Call the school immediately and report that someone is picking on your child.
   2. Lecture him not to play with the bad boy again.
   3. Listen. Find out who was hit first . . . why . . . and how hard.

2. Your child is absorbed in making mudpies outside. You would like her to come in to see a nature special on TV because she will learn something important.
   1. Tell her to get in the house and clean up because you have something worthwhile for her to do.
   2. Decide that she's as close to nature right now as she can get.

3. Your three children have just taken all of the cushions off the couch and are tussling on them.

1. Lose your cool. It's a brand-new couch, and you already set up the no-dismantling rule. All three get in trouble.
2. Redirect them to another activity, giving them the choice of a quiet indoor activity or the opportunity to go outside.
3. Provide some old cushions and let them pounce on them in a specified place where they can't get hurt or hurt anything else.

4. You take the kids on vacation, and on the way home you're happy they remember:
   1. the Grand Canyon.
   2. the Smithsonian Institution.
   3. the comic books they read in the car.
   4. whatever good memory they may have.

(Jasinek & Ryan, 1988)

What do participants say about parent training? "This should be a required class in high school," said one father. Others attend reluctantly. "For some reason they don't want others to know they are having difficulty," a leader observed. "When they come and participate, notwithstanding these problems, I really love it! It's so rewarding to help them and to see the light bulb go on in their heads. I wouldn't trade it for anything."

A clinical psychologist explained:

> If a parent is really serious about relating to his kids and saving his family and he is willing to learn, he can turn things around. I had a divorced father whose thirteen-year-old daughter was hospitalized for drug abuse and emotional problems come to my two-hour family-training workshops twice a week. He was diligent in doing everything he was taught to do, a great example of teachability. Because of the changes he made, his daughter is now off drugs and has developed a strong relationship with him. When a father like him puts his heart and soul into learning how to change, wonderful things can happen.

ACTIVITIES FOR PARENTS AND KIDS

17.1 After each parenting workshop session you attend, meet with your kids to discuss what the highlights were and how they might apply to your family. Family members could also list questions for you to bring up at your next session.

17.2 How important is being right and winning arguments to you and your family? Ask yourself, is making sarcastic, sniping remarks a habit you have developed? If so, how could you work on changing the habit?

REFERENCES

Hanna, Joseph. 1996. "Control Panel." *Los Angeles Times,* August 18, p. E3.
Jasinek, Doris, & Ryan, Pamela Bell. 1988. *How to Build a House of Hearts: A Heart-Level Home Makes Everyone Who Lives There Feel Good.* Minneapolis: CompCare Publishers.
Los Angeles Times. 1996. November 10, p. D5.
Morrow, Jeffrey S. 1994. "Parent Training Works!" *The Parenting Instructor,* Winter, p. 3.

18 Parent-Support Groups

Raising a rebellious youngster who constantly struggles against reasonable expectations is disheartening. A parent-support group can help you realize that you are a survivor, not a failure. Remember, your child is neither a loser nor your enemy. Nor is it your goal to seek revenge.

Getting together with other parents who are experiencing similar problems can help. Working together on common problems can buoy you up and carry you through difficult times. You will experience relief knowing that you aren't the only parent who is struggling. The more you help one another, the stronger and wiser you will become.

"Parenting is mostly trial and error," a support-group participant remembered. "The group helps you when you are inexperienced and new to a problem. The leaders try to balance out newcomers with those who've been there for a while—so there's a blend."

Sidebar 18.1: Toughlove Support Group

When you go to the TOUGHLOVE group, you'll see:

> people just like you,
> people struggling to change,
> people excited by their own accomplishments,
> people reaching out to help each other,
> people admitting their fears and failures,
> people who will see right through your B.S.,
> people who will be there when you need them,
> people who will expect you to be there for them,
> people giving,
> people getting,
> people who know where you've been,
> people who know where you're going, and
> people whose lives are getting better (York & York, 1984).

A parent-support group also neutralizes the unhealthy power of the school-based adolescent-peer network. Kids get together on a daily basis and pool information, and some scheme about ways to manipulate and control. This social networking gives them an advantage over their parents. When parents organize, the adolescent-peer group has less power. Knowledge and unity equal power.

Support Group Format

If there isn't a parent-support group in your area, start one. Let other parents know about your group by telling school principals, religious leaders, and youth counselors. Start small by meeting in a home. As the group becomes larger, move to a community center, public school, or other building such as a church or synagogue.

Begin with a brief (about fifteen minutes) introductory meeting to introduce new parents and make announcements, then divide into smaller groups for about one and a half hours. (Six couples in each group is ideal.) Form new units as your numbers grow. Select a facilitator in each unit to ensure that every parent has an opportunity to speak. The facilitator usually begins by saying, "Is there anyone in crisis now?" Those parents who are in crisis describe what situation they're facing, what they've done, and how they feel. Other parents listen sympathetically, ask questions, and share experiences with similar problems. This gives beleaguered parents relief and provides encouragement and direction for the coming week.

The other parents then report on their progress. Failure is met with sympathetic understanding—never with criticism—and success with approval and applause.

During the last fifteen minutes, the small units reconvene into the larger group, in which people briefly share victories, to the applause of all participants. If a small unit can't resolve a thorny problem, it might ask the larger group for experiences and solutions. "Each problem situation is unique," one parent remarked, "and the solution must be tailored to the particular circumstances." But the main thing is discussing what works and what doesn't. Ask, "Have you tried this?"

Confidentiality is a *must!* Whatever is said in the meetings remains there. Parents never talk about what happens in the support group in the presence of their offspring or anyone else.

In getting the group started, you may want to ask a professional from the local mental-health center to attend a meeting. He or she could tell participants about community resources and teach you a few principles of behavioral management—the same kinds of skills taught in parent-training workshops. (See Chapter 17.)

Parenting Problems and Solutions

A variety of problems come up in a parent's group. For example, a youngster may continually frustrate his mother by leaving wet towels on the bathroom floor and be secretly pleased when she complains or explodes. "How are we going to take care of this towel problem?" a group leader may ask. Ideally, consequences should be linked to behavior choices. For example, when youngsters abuse a privilege, parents can withdraw the privilege until their kids demonstrate that they can handle the responsibility that goes with the privilege. In this case, parents and teen could develop a contract saying that Mom will provide towels and launder them at no expense to the youngster (the privilege). He, in turn, will hang up the towels after each shower (the responsibility). If he doesn't, the towels disappear, and he can earn them back only by performing chores chosen by Mom (the consequence).

"My sixteen-year-old son's behavior was *way* out of line," a parent reports,

> and he wouldn't follow our family rules. At the recommendation of the parent group, we removed the door from his bedroom, denying him his privacy. We also removed his bed and everything but a sleeping bag and a pillow. At first he thought it was funny, a piece of cake. But after three weeks he started asking when he'd get his bed back. He realized that if he was going to live with us he would have to keep our family rules. He started obeying curfew and acting more civil at home.

Expect your teen to test you to see whether you are going to consistently follow through. Difficult kids have a repertoire of behaviors that keep them in control and keep their parents off balance and emotionally distraught. Support groups diffuse youth control by helping parents understand and manage their emotions by following a rational plan of behavioral management. "Rather than having parents explode in rage at their kids' behavior," a leader explains,

> we encourage them to establish rules—no more than ten—and have kids sign contracts to keep the rules or lose privileges. It specifies consequences for infractions of the rules. The goal is to help them deal with problems without getting all carried away with their emotions.

Make rules that outline specific behaviors simple and reasonable. By writing them down in contract form, parents can think them through clearly and rationally and specify the consequences for compliance or deviance. Follow through consistently, with abundant praise and positive rewards for *any* progress. "It really helps and encourages the parents to reach a common ground, present a united front to the kid with rules—keep them short and simple—and hold down all the emotion," said a group leader.

As parental hostilities mount, so does an inclination to retaliate with physical or emotional abuse. As you regain control of your home, beware of swinging too far toward toughness. Programs that overemphasize punishment at the expense of positive rewards substitute one problem for another. Make your discipline consistent and reasonable, and provide it calmly, not in anger.

No youngster in control at home will willingly give up this power. As parents begin to discipline by enforcing consequences, offspring will likely rant and rave. Years of experience teach astute youngsters how to "push buttons" to upset and manipulate their parents. Do not meet emotional outbursts in kind. Simply say, "I'll discuss this with you when you calm down," then turn and walk away. Shouting matches help no one and only worsen the problem.

A single mom told her support group that her verbally abusive son took the family car after a heated exchange—in spite of a clearly posted house rule that the car was not to be used without permission. "Did you call the cops?" asked a group member. "No," she answered. "Is he on your insurance policy?" another asked. "Are you aware that if he crashed and killed someone, your car would be impounded and you held liable?" Again, "Nope." Everyone looked around in silence, and then, as if in chorus, the other parents said "The Club" [a steering-wheel lock]. "Purchase 'The Club' so it is impossible for him to take your car again."

Keeping records of inappropriate behaviors sometimes helps. The daughter of one couple, in anger, called her stepfather a "faggot" and reported him to public officials as a child molester. "All he would do is look at her and she'd report him," a leader remembered.

> When the social workers came to investigate, the couple produced a notebook logging the daughter's incorrigible behavior over a four- to five-month period. After about twenty minutes of reading this and spending ten minutes with the girl, the social workers left. Our group had encouraged these parents to keep this log to protect themselves against this type of stunt and to vent their anger on paper rather than on their daughter.

Like parent-training workshops, parent-support groups can also benefit a marriage by bringing spouses together in a mutual child-rearing plan. Living with an out-of-control youngster often pits one parent against the other, as one becomes permissive ("loving") and the other tough. In these homes, it is easy for teens to manipulate and control parents. Other parents in your support group can often see to the heart of your problems and help you become more united. "As a small-group facilitator," a father noted, the biggest problem I saw was when one parent was very autocratic—hard lined—and the other one was easy. The kid played one parent off against the other and was able to get away with it. Our group brought the parents together to present a united front to the kid, letting him know he couldn't pull off his old tricks. And it took all the negative emotion out of things.

Parents can support each other between meetings as well. Distribute participants' names and phone numbers. Remember: Don't give kids access to this list! A member of the support group can encourage parents, by phone, to be firm, deal with guilt feelings in a productive way, and restrain themselves from denying their youngster the opportunity to learn from the natural consequences of their behavior.

Sidebar 18.2: Finding Support

Anyone who is trying to change needs support. Support can come in all these forms:

> hand holding
> confronting
> saying encouraging things
> talking over difficult tasks
> suggesting new directions
> being tough
> praising
> being there

Support is a two-way street: giving and getting.

Support includes sharing yourself with others when they need help.

Support is what helps you face yourself, step out, change, and cause change.

Support helps you to become competent.

Support prevents loneliness.

Support is the way you will become powerful.

Support is the basis for cooperation.

Support helps you manage tension.

Support helps you cope with pain.

Support is doing what another may find too difficult.

Support is really listening to another person.

Support is real friendship.

Support is sharing.

Support lets you move in a direction you would like to go.

Support helps you stop old behavior.

Support lets you start new behavior.

Support helps you make changes that last (York & York, 1984, p. 44–45).

A single mother with an adolescent son who towers over her may occasionally need help from fathers in her support group. Their role, of course, is not to harass her son, but simply to show up at critical times to demonstrate the mother's strength and resources. "Once we sent two adult men over to help her when he was bullying her around. It strengthened her position and gave her some much needed clout."

"We saw a lot of successes, some major," a parent remarked. "But the most encouraging were the small ones, just an inkling that things were turning around. That's when everyone was encouraged to continue." "But we had some failures too," another parent commented. "One dad who was very autocratic wasn't willing to lighten up or back off. He wasn't willing to listen or change, so his situation continued to get worse."

"Parents need all the help they can get," a group leader emphasized.

> In this complex world, kids are exposed to a lot of garbage. Our son went to a school with some pretty raunchy fellows. But with our parent-group we got him away from them. When I ask him now [several years later] about some of these kids, he says he hasn't seen them at all and doesn't plan to. He's always been smart and hard working, so now that he's on his own he's reaping some of the benefits of clean living. I continually congratulate him on his successes.

ACTIVITIES FOR PARENTS AND KIDS

18.1 Discuss why parents might find a support group useful. Consider the following analogy: Just as athletes can improve their game by talking and working out with other athletes, parents can become better at parenting by exchanging ideas with other parents.

18.2 Without compromising confidentiality, bring up topics from your support group for family discussion. Explain that you value input from family members, just as you do from fellow parents in the ongoing quest to strengthen your family.

REFERENCES

York, Phyllis, & York, David. 1996. *Toughlove: A Self-Help Manual for Kids in Trouble*. P.O. Box 1069, Doylestown, PA 18901.

19 Family Therapy

By the time chemical dependency claims a family member, the entire family is in crisis. Typically everyone develops a dysfunctional role that reinforces the problem and perpetuates a downward spiral. Avoid any therapist who will not involve you in the treatment process. "I never take on a troubled child whose parents are not involved in the therapy," said one practitioner. "When a parent asks me to 'fix' the child, I always explain that I can't help without dealing with the entire family. The parents need to participate." He explains: "Often the parents are in denial about their own problems and are using the kid as a scapegoat. I help them deal with their own issues. They may be struggling in their marriage or covering up family secrets such as alcoholism, drug addiction, or spousal abuse."

Getting the Right Help

One six-year-old boy started exhibiting behavior problems in school—not of a severe nature, mostly socially withdrawing or acting inappropriately. So, his parents rushed him off to weekly appointments with a psychiatrist. Many "colored pictures" and thousands of dollars later, I asked the mom how her son was getting along in his individual counseling sessions. She replied, "I don't know, it's between him and his therapist." I was astounded that there had been no family involvement with her son's treatment. A probation officer once criticized this approach, saying, "It's like taking a child out of a dirty puddle, cleaning him up, and then tossing him back into the puddle. We need to deal with the puddle, not just the child."

Most of us usually don't seek professional therapy until we feel we can no longer cope with our problems on our own. At such times, our primary concern is survival—physical and emotional. The process preceding the crisis usually goes like this: We naively assume that chemical dependency can never happen in our family, and we overlook and deny or "normalize" the indications. When we do recognize the problem, we may deny its extent and severity, and we don't know how to proceed. Next, we try to control the problem by making angry threats or punishing the user. When these efforts prove futile, we alternate between depression, anger, and guilt. We fear our future and judge ourselves as parental failures. When our best efforts to solve the problem prove ineffective, family morale sinks until everyone gives up, or hopes that the chemically dependent person will leave or die. Only when neither occur do some of us reach out for help. Anger and hurt replace the love and concern we once felt for the drug user.

Family therapy can halt this scenario, restore hope, and teach participants how to interact in more positive and healthy ways. A family therapist remembered,

> I try to help parents realize how fragile and insecure we are at birth—fear and insecurity are our most primitive feelings—and how important it is for parents to provide a loving and secure abode for children. I help them develop a simple formula for success: love plus firm boundaries equal a healthy abode.

Healthy Families

This list of traits of a healthy family comes from a survey of more than 550 professionals who work with families:

- Healthy families communicate well. They listen reflectively rather than defensively and pay attention to nonverbal communications, particularly silences and touches. Healthy families occasionally quarrel, accept the fact that they may not always agree, and are able to reconcile their differences through discussion. In contrast, unhealthy families let quarrels go on without making up.

Sidebar 19.1: Secrets of Effective Communication

Listening Skills

1. *The Disarming Technique.* You find some truth in what the other person is saying, even if you feel convinced that what they're saying is totally wrong, unreasonable, irrational, or unfair.

2. *Empathy.* You put yourself in the other person's shoes and try to see the world through his or her eyes.
   - *Thought empathy:* You paraphrase the other person's words.
   - *Feeling empathy:* You acknowledge how they're probably feeling, given what they say to you.

3. *Inquiry:* You ask gentle, probing questions to learn more about what the other person is thinking and feeling.

Self-Expression Skills

1. *"I feel" statements.* You express your feelings with "I feel" statements (such as "I feel upset") rather than with "you" statements (such as "You're wrong!" or "You're making me furious!").
2. *Stroking:* You find something genuinely positive to say to the other person, even in the heat of battle. This indicates that you respect the other person, even though you may be angry with each other (Burns, 1989, p. 377).

■ Healthy families also display mutual affirmation and emotional support to foster individual self-esteem. They respect and value individual differences. Unhealthy families, on the other hand, give more respect to high achievers (athletes, scholars, etc.). Members of healthy families trust one another: Spouses trust each other's marital fidelity, parents trust their children with responsibilities, and children trust their parents to provide acceptance and nurturing.

Sidebar 19.2: Conditional Parental Acceptance

"I had a hard time feeling that I amounted to much," an addict remembers, "but alcohol took that feeling away. My Dad was never home and everything was black and white. I was supposed to get good grades and not play."

■ Healthy families also have a constructive sense of humor and play together. Although they experience stressful circumstances, humor diffuses the tension inherent in explosive situations. Unhealthy families use humor destructively in sarcasm and put-downs.
■ Healthy families share responsibilities, teach the difference between right and wrong, and have a strong sense of family traditions. Interaction is balanced between all members, not focused intensively in subgroups (such as between mother and daughter). Such families often have a shared religious core that may or may not be oriented to a specific church or synagogue. They respect one another's privacy and value service to others, although they avoid excessive volunteerism.
■ Healthy families foster regular dinner-time conversation, and share some, but not all, leisure time. They also seek outside help when problems arise (Curran, 1983).

Emotionally Impaired Families

Of course, there are no perfect families, and all of us can improve. "I think everybody's family is dysfunctional in some regard, many more so than others," a recovering addict speculates, "but I am sure family health varies by degree."

Sidebar 19.3: How Do Healthy Families Work?

Healthy families are not perfect; they may have yelling, bickering, misunderstanding, tension, hurt, and anger—but not all the time. In healthy families emotional expression is allowed and accepted. Family members can freely ask for and give attention. Rules are explicit and remain consistent, but with some flexibility to adapt to individual needs and particular situations. Healthy families allow for individuality; each member is encouraged to pursue his or her own interests, and boundaries between individuals are honored.

Children are consistently treated with respect, and do not fear emotional, verbal, physical, or sexual abuse. Parents can be counted on to provide care for their children. Children are given responsibilities appropriate to their age and are not expected to take on parental responsibilities. Finally, in healthy families everyone makes mistakes; mistakes are allowed. Perfection is unattainable, unrealistic, and potentially dull and sterile (Lambert, 1997).

Affection is displayed in dysfunctional families in unusual ways, as this addict attests.

I came from a bunch of crackpots where there was no affection or socializing. Rather than expressing affection, my parents paid for everything I did. Even now I can't visit my mother without her handling me a ten-dollar bill. It's ridiculous. When I was a teenager, I wanted to get out of there as fast as I could.

In such homes children become numb to feelings—"I learned to stuff my feelings." Often, they are taught to maintain family secrets at all costs and not to show pain. Kids in such an environment can easily fall into drug-abusing lifestyles, which provide highs from chemicals rather than parental love. "As a child I was unloved and felt unlovable," one user remembers.

I had a feeling of inferiority and felt that I was less than other people and didn't fit in. But when I took a drink or did drugs, all those feelings left. I could interact with other people and feel as good on the inside as others looked like they were on the outside.

Sidebar 19.4: Characteristics of Bad Communication

- *Truth.* You insist that you are "right" and the other person is "wrong."
- *Blame.* You say that the problem is the other person's fault.
- *Martyrdom.* You claim that you're an innocent victim.
- *Put-down.* You imply that the other person is a loser because he or she "always" or "never" does certain things.
- *Hopelessness.* You give up and insist there's no point in trying.
- *Demandingness.* You say you're entitled to better treatment but you refuse to ask for what you want in a direct, straightforward way.
- *Denial.* You insist that you don't feel angry, hurt, or sad when you really do.
- *Passive Aggression.* You pout or withdraw or say nothing. You may storm out of the room or slam doors.
- *Self-blame.* Instead of dealing with the problem, you act as if you're an awful, terrible person.
- *Helping.* Instead of hearing how depressed, hurt, or angry the other person feels, you try to "solve the problem" or "help" him or her.
- *Sarcasm.* Your words or tone of voice convey tension or hostility which you aren't openly acknowledging.
- *Scapegoating.* You suggest that the other person has "a problem" and that you're sane, happy, and uninvolved in the conflict.
- *Defensiveness.* You refuse to admit any wrong-doing or imperfection.
- *Counterattack.* Instead of acknowledging how the other person feels, you respond to their criticism by criticizing them.
- *Diversion.* Instead of dealing with how you both feel in the here-and-now, you list grievances about past injustices (Burns, 1989, p. 365).

Dysfunctional families generally have at least one person, usually a parent, who plays the role of an *enabler*. This person is constantly on a rescue mission, protecting and sheltering the drug user from the natural consequences of his or her behavior. It is easy to fall into this role with our adolescents. After all, only a few years ago they were totally dependent on us, helpless infants, and our role was to provide them with protection and care. Although enablers' actions stem from loving intentions, they actually reinforce the manipulative skills the drug user has retained from infancy. When the user "cries," the enabling parent "jumps" to protect his or her "baby." Because we take our parental responsibility seriously, a kid's drug use threatens our sense of competence and worth as parents.

It's easy to become preoccupied with a problem youngster. However, this preoccupation can hurt our relationships with other family members and friends. Also, it is not much fun being an enabler. Rather than appreciating the help a troubled teen usually resents it. The harder the enabler tries, the worse things become. Indeed, in Synanon Center, a drug rehabilitation program, addicts in treatment disdainfully use the term "mother lover" to rebuke anyone who enables another's bad behavior.

When we lie to friends and other family members about youngsters' drug use or in any way support them in their use, we foolishly shield them from the consequences of their behavior and thus delay their recovery. When we feel responsible for others' feelings and well-being and assume that it is our obligation to meet their every need, we rob them of their sense of choice and accountability. When we allow them to control our emotions, we become "codependent" with them in their self-defeating behaviors. Parental codependency reaches its nadir when we blame ourselves for our children's bad choices, take full responsibility for their behavior, and try to cover up their mistakes.

A good family therapist will help an enabling parent realize that he has not caused his child's problem, nor can he control or cure it. But he can learn to cope with it. Family therapy will help parents be appropriately supportive, without shouldering the responsibility for "fixing" others' problems.

In addition to enablers, other members in dysfunctional families also adopt specific roles; they are pigeon-holed into one of these scripts:

- *The Doer.* Provides most or all of the maintenance functions in the family, makes sure the kids are dressed and fed, pays the bills, irons the shirts, cooks dinner, takes the kids to baseball practice and violin lessons. Because that's about all that the Doer has the time or energy to do, he or she feels tired, lonely, taken advantage of, neglected, and empty—but also gets a lot of satisfaction out of being so accomplished. The Doer's own unhealthy sense of guilt and overdeveloped sense of responsibility keep him or her going.
- *The Lost Child.* Deals with the family dysfunction by escaping. This is the child (or parent) who stays in her room a lot, or the one who goes out to the woods to play by himself. A deep loneliness pervades those who fill this role.
- *The Hero.* Provides self-esteem for the family. He carries the family banner for all the public to see and makes the family proud—but at a terrible price in terms of his own well-being.
- *The Mascot.* Often one of the younger children; provides humor and comic relief for the family, giving the family a sense of fun, playfulness, or silliness. The cost to the Mascot is that his or her true feelings of pain and isolation never get expressed, and he remains an emotional cripple until he gets into therapy.

- *The Saint/Priest/Nun/Rabbi.* The child who expresses the family's spirituality and atones for family sins. Although the expectation is rarely spoken, the child is subtly molded to believe that his or her worth comes only from acting out the family's spirituality by becoming a priest, etc.
- *The Scapegoat.* Acts out all of the family's dysfunction and takes the blame for the family. The "black sheep," he gets drug addicted or steals, gets in fights, acts out sexually, etc. The family then gets to say, "If little brother weren't such a delinquent, we'd be a healthy family." The social and emotional cost to the Scapegoat is obvious.
- *Daddy's Little Princess/Mommy's Little Man.* Gets to be "a little spouse" to one of the parents. Although this privileged role feels good to the child, it is a form of "emotional or covert incest." That is, the child does not get a chance to be a child and is seduced into this role by a parent who is too afraid or emotionally impaired to get his or her needs met by another adult. Many who adopt this role may wind up physically or emotionally abused by others in their adult relationships (Friel & Friel, 1988).

Therapeutic Approaches

Many family therapists use an educational approach rather than a medical model. Instead of providing "therapy" (which may seem to imply that clients are sick or have failed), the therapist adopts an instructor's role, teaching social skills to enhance success inside and outside the home. Find a competent, caring therapist. Research the matter as thoroughly as you would to find a new doctor or dentist. If your family feels consistently uncomfortable with the therapist, find a better fit.

Therapists generally target specific behaviors for change and teach more appropriate behaviors. Working with the entire family, the therapist encourages youths and parents to set goals and teaches parents to provide positive reinforcement (attention, acceptance, praise, and other rewards). "Only in extreme cases will I see a family more than once a week," said a therapist.

> This is because I require families to make an investment in the outcome by doing a lot of homework. If I see that they express a lot of criticism, I assign them to break this destructive habit by, for example, giving at least one compliment each day. If they have trouble expressing emotion, I may assign them to hug daily and to keep a record of their feelings.

Family interventions using an educational approach avoid stigmatizing assumptions. The approach is positive rather than negative, educational rather than punitive, and preventive rather than remedial. Such an approach helps parents let go of guilt and shame and invest energies in positive actions.

ACTIVITIES FOR PARENTS AND KIDS

19.1 Try some of the "getting to know you" board games on the market. Provide a good way for family members to share feelings, memories, and laughter.

19.2 Discuss the "Secrets of Effective Communication" (Sidebar 19.1). Give *positive* examples of family members or acquaintances using these skills. Practice some of them in a simulated (role play) situation.

19.3 Read "How Do Healthy Families Work?" in Sidebar 19.3. How important it is for your family members to:

- be perfect,
- express emotion,
- have reasonable and clearly defined roles,
- freely ask for and give attention,
- pursue own interests and express individualism,
- honor privacy and boundaries between family members,
- treat each other with respect,
- avoid hurtful criticism of one another,
- allow mistakes,
- praise one another,
- enjoy family activities and go places together,
- keep family secrets,
- laugh together,
- eat together,
- go on family vacations.

REFERENCES

Burns, David D. 1989. *The Feeling Good Handbook*. New York: Plume Books.

Curran, Delores. 1983. *Traits of a Healthy Family*. San Francisco: Harper and Row.

Friel, John and Linda Friel. 1988. *Adult Children, The Secrets of Dysfunctional Families*. Deerfield, FL: Health Communications, Inc.

Lambert, Dorinda J. 1997. "Dysfunctional Families: Recognizing and Overcoming Their Effects." Kansas State University, University Counseling Services. [modified for the internet: www.ksu.edu/ucs/dysfunc.html].

20 Twelve-Step Programs

Recovering from chemical dependency can take a long time and may require active long-term involvement in a support system such as Alcoholics Anonymous (AA) or Narcotics Anonymous (NA). These groups—some of them exclusively for teens—provide unconditional acceptance and a twelve-step program of healing. They have helped countless people throughout the world to overcome compulsive behaviors. "The twelve-step program is the best option available," asserted a treatment specialist addicted as a teenager. "It is group therapy at its finest. Time tested for decades, it has helped lots of people stay sober. I've seen miracles. There's no doubt in my mind that without it I, for one, would be dead today."

Sidebar 20.1: Alcoholics Anonymous' Effectiveness

Seven directors of the United States' drug-control program from five presidential administrations met in 1994 to review past accomplishments in the war on drugs and ideas for future strategies. Robert L. Du Pont (from the Nixon administration), regretting his slowness in realizing the worth of the twelve-step approach, called it "the secret weapon in the war on drugs. It is completely free; there is no bureaucrat involved; there is no hungry mouth to feed; it can't be cut out of anybody's budget; it can't go out of fashion; and it is accessible to every single person all the time" ("Reflections of the Drug Czars," 1995, p. 222).

Alcoholics Anonymous

AA's only requirement for membership is the desire to stop drinking or abusing other drugs. There are no dues or fees; groups are self-supporting through member contributions. Nor is AA allied with any political, religious, business, or civic organization. Its only purpose is to keep members clean and sober.

Participants are encouraged to attend meetings at whatever frequency they need—weekly, daily, or even hourly. Meetings are conducted by a leader who introduces himself or herself and encourages attendees to do likewise—on a first-name basis to protect anonymity. Individuals have the opportunity to share their stories, ask for help, or give support and guidance to others based on their own experiences. Most participants feel a strong commitment to attend these meetings regularly.

The twelve-step approach can also significantly help family members of chemically dependent people through Al-Anon, a parallel organization for those whose lives are adversely affected by an alcoholic or drug user. Working the twelve steps helps participants focus on their own development and deal more successfully with the recovering alcoholic or addict.

Sidebar 20.2: Alcoholics Anonymous' Twelve Steps

The fundamental principles of recovery in AA's twelve-steps are:

1. We admitted we were powerless over alcohol—that our lives had become unmanageable.
2. Came to believe that a Power greater than ourselves could restore us to sanity.
3. Made a decision to turn our will and our lives over to the care of God as we understood Him.
4. Made a searching and fearless moral inventory of ourselves.
5. Admitted to God, to ourselves and to another human being the exact nature of our wrongs.
6. Were entirely ready to have God remove all these defects of character.
7. Humbly asked him to remove our shortcomings.
8. Made a list of all persons we had harmed, and became willing to make amends to them all.
9. Made direct amends to such people wherever possible, except when to do so would injure them or others.
10. Continued to take personal inventory and when we were wrong promptly admitted it.
11. Sought through prayer and meditation to improve our conscious contact with God, as we understood Him, praying only for knowledge of His will for us and the power to carry that out.
12. Having had a spiritual awakening as the result of these steps, we tried to carry this message to alcoholics and to practice these principles in all our affairs (Alcoholics Anonymous, 1976).

This addicted teenager's story illustrates how he became an alcoholic and how AA, which offered the original twelve-step program, can help.

"When I was a sophomore in high school, I was already into the early stage of alcoholism," Jim recalled.

Football season was over, so I scored a six-pack of beer and started drinking. I loved the euphoric feeling it gave me. When people came to class to talk about the evils of alcohol I'd think, "This isn't bad; it's great! I love it!"

Jim's life gradually slid downhill. First, his peer group changed. "I moved from the crowd who wasn't into partying to one with people who liked to drink the way I did," he recalled. Next his grades and athletic performance declined.

When people started mentioning that I might have a drinking problem, I began working extra hard to excel at school and in sports so I could tell them, "How could I be doing so well if I had a drinking problem? It's ridiculous!"

Jim regarded his drinking as manly.

I thought a man was supposed to be able to drink a lot, and I took a lot of pride in being able to drink anybody under the table—the great American folklore. It felt really good when people would say, "Wow, Jim, it's amazing how you can put all this stuff away." It boosted my ego.

His body built up a tolerance, and physical symptoms appeared. "I noticed that the next morning the withdrawal was a bit more than what the other guys experienced. I had little shakes and sweats but it hadn't progressed to the DTs yet." His blackouts caused him some concern.

I would wake up the next morning not remembering things that had happened. My life was like a slide-projector show. I could tell you where I was in the slides but I didn't have the slightest idea how I got from one to the next.

Other problems quickly followed. His girlfriend left him when she tired of his drinking, and this became a justification to drink more. "You'd get loaded too if you had to deal with that kind of stuff," he reasoned.

I rationalized to the point that I truly believed my lies. I was all clouded and deluded and totally preoccupied with where the next drink was, whose house the party was at, whose parents are going to be gone, where can we get liquor where they don't card us [check for identification]—all of that business.

To further prove his critics wrong, he sought counsel from others, hoping for reassurance that he was not an alcoholic. "I went to an Episcopal priest and said, 'I think I may have a problem with alcohol.' He replied, 'Oh, no, you're too young to be an alcoholic.' Oh, what a relief!" Athletic coaches also confirmed that anyone who played as well as he did couldn't possibly have a drinking problem.

During these early years, parents and friends usually covered for him when he got into trouble—which happened often, for he frequently drove under the influence. He recalled with embarrassment that, for his first mug-shot in jail, he had his athletic letterman's jacket on. "My parents tried to cover up the embarrassment I caused them," he remembered. "When they met their neighbors at a party and started bragging about their children's achievements, my parents would say, 'Oh, he's working for the County right now.' Actually I was in the County Jail."

Jim's problems escalated at college, where he was away from parental control. "I let loose and became a full-bore alcoholic," he recounted.

> When people would say, "You really need help with this stuff," I'd say "I'm too young to be an alcoholic. Alcoholics are old skid-row bums." My male ego wouldn't let me believe that this bottle—one that I could break into a billion pieces—was actually breaking me. So, I developed plans to change my drinking pattern—switching drinks, or not drinking on certain days, all that stuff. But once I started, I couldn't quit. I just kept drinking.

By the time Jim was twenty-two he had rolled two cars. One day he passed out behind the wheel at an intersection, backing up traffic for blocks. "That's when the moment of clarity came," he recalled. "Either I was going to have to get help, or this was going to be my life." His family and friends evidently came to the same conclusion. "My parents stopped bailing me out of jail and covering up for me when I passed out. They'd had it with me, so now I had to deal with the consequences of my drinking."

This development, plus legal troubles, left Jim little choice but to get help. The judge "gave me a get-well card," he recalled. "I call it the 'nudge from the judge.'" Among the things the judge required was that Jim attend AA meetings. "I remember thinking that AA was for winos who met in dingy basements—a bunch of people in Columbo raincoats hanging out with their bottles." Nonetheless, he had little choice but to go along. "I thought I'd do what I had to do to get these people off my butt, and then I'd go back to drinking the way I wanted to."

Sidebar 20.3: How to Find a Twelve-Step Group for Teenagers

- Look under "Drug Abuse and Addiction Information and Treatment Centers" in the Yellow Pages of your telephone directory, and call agencies in your area that deal with mental-health problems.
- Call the Central Office for Alcoholics Anonymous (AA) in your area. (You can find it by looking in the White Pages of your

telephone directory. Call and ask for a directory of AA meetings in your area.) Also, look for "Young People's Groups" (marked with a designation "Y.P.").

■ Call your area hospital and ask for the inpatient pediatric or adolescent unit or their social-work office. They should have appropriate referrals for teenage alcohol and drug problems.

■ Check for Teen-Anon in the telephone book, or visit www.teen-anon.com on the Internet. (More on Teen-Anon later in this chapter.)

At AA, Jim was surprised to find people who, though dissimilar in backgrounds, shared feelings and experiences similar to his own.

People painted all kinds of pictures about what got them there, but their blackouts and feelings were the same—fear, anger, guilt, and remorse. I came to recognize that my false pride and male ego were doing me under and decided to flush them down the drain. The hardest part was getting honest with myself about what I was doing. I had to abandon a whole book of lies, excuses, and rationales about why I drank. It was hard for me to admit that I couldn't handle this stuff. When I heard that addiction is a lonely person's disease, I understood completely because I had alienated so many people. I *really* wanted to belong someplace. Once I started listening with my heart, I started to have hope that I could come back from the shell of the person I had become.

Progress was slow for Jim. "The first year I wasn't even sure where I had landed, but I wanted most of all to feel normal—and here I was with a group of people where it is normal *not* to drink." And their acceptance of him was gratifying. "There was such a wonderful warmth there," he marveled.

You walk into a meeting, and you are greeted with loving and caring people who are genuinely concerned. They all understand what it is like to walk in for the first time, so they shine this loving light on you, so to speak, and they never remove it. And then you learn how to do the same for others. All of a sudden the world doesn't focus on you anymore, and you find out that you can grow by giving away what you've been given. What a terrific blueprint for happy living.

Recovering addicts also share a common understanding. "Communicating with people who have been through it before is the only thing that works," one emphasized.

I can remember when I was worried about going to jail. There was a lawyer in our group who had been incarcerated and gotten his life back on track. He talked to me from a deep well of experience that no one else could provide because he had been there and knew what it was like.

Living by the principles of AA—working the twelve steps—involves laborious and often painful individual effort, such as cataloging all one's drug-related foibles and discussing them in a support group. This is how one participant described the process: "First you admit that you have a problem, go through the inventory process, and share that inventory with another person. Then you make restitution, continue to treat people right, and help others in their recovery."

Working the steps can be difficult, and relapses do occur. However, in the long run, AA may be the best, even the only, way out of the abyss for addicts. As one former addict explained:

> Before I found AA I had seen seven psychiatrists, five psychologists, and four drug and alcohol counselors. I had done transactional analysis, Jungian, Reichian, and Freudian therapy. I had tried transcendental meditation, biofeedback, hypnosis, and self-hypnosis. But in all those twelve years of therapy, I never breathed a sober breath. I now refer to myself as a survivor of the mental-health system. Unfortunately, no one ever mentioned to me twelve-step programs such as AA or NA until the very end, when I began my recovery. The therapists thought that I drank because of my behavior and my mental illness. They always had the cart before the horse (Coombs, 1997, p. 222).

Twelve-step programs provide peer support, an extraordinarily important recovery tool, by matching each new member with a sponsor—someone of the same gender who has been in AA for a longer time. The new member can call on this person twenty-four hours a day.

> You're given a sponsor, a travel guide and mentor who knows the territory. You stick close to him for the first couple of years, just like he's another parent, and you ask him, "Should I do this or that?" (Coombs, 1997, p. 219).

Your entire family can directly benefit from AA activities. AA invites family members to such activities as open meetings to hear AA speakers or to share in the fellowship with other families. Social events (suppers, dances, picnics, and other activities) are held regularly for AA members and their families, as are weekend conferences at resorts and hotels. Al-Anon and Alateen meetings for family members are often held concurrently at these conferences.

Teen-Anon Recovery

Teen-Anon (not the same as Ala-teen), a national nonprofit twelve-step fellowship, helps kids ages twelve to nineteen who are experiencing problems with drugs—and those who love them. Groups of kids meet for ninety minutes one or more times each week to address the life skills, self-esteem, and co-dependency issues specific to teens in recovery.

The core structure is based on its twelve-step forerunners, Alcoholics Anonymous and Narcotics Anonymous. But because kids have unique life circumstances, needs, and problems, Teen-Anon is more structured and comprehensive in addressing vital areas of teen development, such as anger management, conflict resolution, creative-strategic thinking, and self-esteem enhancement. Unlike twelve-step groups for adults, Teen-Anon groups are led by qualified adult volunteers: counselors, therapists, teachers or youth leaders. Each group has a youth member as meeting chair and "secretary."

Teen-Anon is not about adults telling teenagers what to do or not do, nor is it about following rules generated by parents or teachers, but learning about healthy living. Its goal is to help kids support each other as they heal from the pain of addiction.

Recovery doesn't stop with being clean, as all recovering addicts learn. Kids who start abstaining from drugs experience profoundly uncomfortable feelings and adjustment problems. Many try to deal with these alone, but find it to be an overwhelming task. Typically, these kids continue with the same friends, switch to another drug and regress into their pathological predicament. It's much more effective for them to find a group of people who support their abstinence—people who have also struggled with addiction and know what they are going through.

Due to stigma, ignorance of treatment options, too few treatment slots, or prohibitive costs, teens with substance abuse problems rarely seek treatment. Teen-Anon offers a no-cost, very available program as well as vital aftercare for successful recovery after treatment. And it focuses on prevention as well as rehabilitation.

The pioneering work for Teen-Anon was done by Streetcats Foundation, a non-profit organization in Oakland, California (267 Lester Avenue, Suite 104, Oakland, CA 94606; www.teen-anon.com, yes@aol.com; phone 510-444-6074) that also operates the National Children's Coalition, one of the nation's largest youth group networking and volunteer placement organizations. Streetcats also co-sponsors (with the National Childrens Coalition—www.child.net) Young & Recovering, a national twelve-step fellowship for twenty-somethings recovering from the abuse of alcohol and other psychoactive drugs. (Contact the latter by e-mailing youngandrecovering@yahoo.com, visiting their Web site at www.youngandrecovering.8k.com or writing to Streetcats Foundation, YA at P.O. Box 191396, San Francisco, CA 94119).

You can reach Teen-Anon at their toll-free number (877-823-TEEN) and log onto their Web site (teen-anon.com) for general information about youth problems and information about starting a group if there isn't one in your area. There is a separate Web site just for Teen-Anon group leaders and a General Recovery Zone Web site with additional material about substance abuse, prevention, treatment and its effects on the family. The Teen-Anon sites are linked to Child.net, Streetcats Foundation's national Web site and to Teensurfer.com, Streetcats Web site just for teenagers.

ACTIVITIES FOR PARENTS AND KIDS

20.1 Visit the Web sites for Alateen (www.al-anon.org/alateen.html) and Al Anon (www.al-anon.org) on the Internet, and discuss the most interesting materials you find there at the dinner table.

20.2 Review each of AA's twelve steps. Can you use any in your family?

REFERENCES

Alcoholics Anonymous. 1976. 3rd edition. New York: Alcoholics Anonymous World Services, Inc.

Coombs, Robert H. 1997. *Drug-Impaired Professionals.* Cambridge, MA: Harvard University Press.

"Reflections of the Drug Czars." 1995. *Prevention Pipeline* (Center for Substance Abuse Prevention), March/April: pp. 117–120.

INTERNET SOURCE

www.teen-anon.com

21 Drug-Treatment Programs

When your teen is out of control and everything else has failed, consider a treatment program. Structured rehabilitation in a controlled environment will give you relief and may help your youngster get off drugs. How do you choose the best treatment option? That depends on your child, your financial situation, and your overall family needs. Investigate various facilities about their staff qualifications and program design. Ask for references from parents whose youngsters have been through the program, and seek their advice and experiences.

Drug-treatment facilities fall into two categories—outpatient and residential. Both use detoxification ("detox") to reduce their clients' physical dependence on drugs. Outpatient drug-free programs may consist of crisis-intervention centers where users in distress can turn for help. They include walk-in centers, twenty-four-hour telephone hotlines, "crash pads" providing emergency living space, and referral centers. They deal with overdoses, help during "bad trips," and offer other short-term services. Crisis-intervention centers are often staffed by nonprofessionals with whom clients relate well.

Other drug-free outpatient programs include psychotherapy and counseling. Counseling with abusers, the most common intervention, may involve a wide variety of techniques, such as behavior therapy, biofeedback, and hypnosis.

Sidebar 21.1: Drug Treatment Saves Money

Treatment is seven times more cost effective in cutting cocaine demand than local law enforcement, eleven times more effective than border interdiction (trying to keep drugs from entering the country), and twenty-two times more effective than efforts to control foreign drug production (Mecca, 1994).

Selecting a Drug-Treatment Program

To find a reliable residential program, look for these characteristics:

Drug-free environment. The staff must have a strong commitment to keeping the environment drug-free. Because drug-using kids are highly skilled at outwitting officials, ask about the safeguards that protect the treatment center from drug infiltration. (One young user smuggled acid into a treatment program in his contact-lens solution bottle.) Treatment programs located in rural areas surrounded by open spaces may be better able to deter the flow of illicit substances into their facility. "Can you imagine a dealer coming out here to sell a few joints?" asked a rural participant.

Medication-free environment. Avoid programs that use medications to keep kids under control. Although some teenagers with acute psychiatric problems may need medications to correct chemical imbalances, these youths should be in another type of program.

Strong track record. The program should have a good outcome record. Check on its success rate—how many enroll, how many "split," and how many graduate? What is the follow-up success rate?

Clear structure. The program should be carefully structured with reasonable requirements that young participants can clearly understand. Successful programs typically include a well defined system—called a "token economy"—in which participants earn points daily for advancement. A resident can earn points, for example, by getting up on time, doing chores, cleaning her room, going to school, getting good grades, and cooperating with staff and peers. Those who consistently earn points advance to higher levels and get better and better rewards.

Sidebar 21.2: One Family's Experience

"Our son was using drugs and alcohol much more than we had even imagined. His life was completely out of control. He was not going to school. He was in trouble with the law. He had become isolated from our family and old friends. He would leave the house late at night and sometimes not return for days. We got to the point where we would not answer the phone. We were convinced he would be killed or put in jail. We tried different treatment programs, but the only result was that our son developed new friends to get high with. We had no idea how to help him. Fortunately, we found a good drug-treatment program and we believe it literally saved our son's life" (www.tasc.com/charity/khk/homepage.htm).

Continuation of schooling. The program needs a viable accredited school component. It is critical that participating youngsters continue their education or vocational training. Succeeding in school is like career success for an adult. There is simply no substitute. An accredited program of quality instruction is essential. Ideally, the school will advance youngsters for mastering course objectives, not for just putting in "seat time."

Appropriate activities. The program should be directed to the age, interests, and special problems of your youngster. Avoid programs that keep young people confined indoors for long periods in passive activities. Teenagers require adventure and big-muscle activities. Some rural, residential drug-treatment programs provide activities such as horsemanship, fishing, water sports, wilderness experiences, animal care, crafts, winter activities, and vocational skills (farming, ranching, milking cows, driving tractors, gardening, etc.). "When youths come into this program," a counselor relates,

> they don't immediately start school—that's a reward they must earn. We put them to work on the farm—we have a big barn and lots of animals—and they spend time feeding animals, herding cows, tending to chickens, rabbits, pigeons, and other birds and animals. This creates good feelings within them. When they decide they *want* to go to school, they start school. We don't hurry them. In other words, when they arrive, our first purpose is to help them feel successful in something. No matter what level they are on, *kids need to succeed!* Feeding animals is an automatic success experience. They put the hay or grain there and in five minutes it's gone. They're helping animals grow, and it's *real* work, needed work, not made-up work.

Some programs start incoming teens with a two-week wilderness experience. Under the supervision of skilled leaders, the kids "rough it out" in the wilderness. Here youngsters learn the importance of preparation and planning and the value of the comforts provided at home. If they haven't made their shelter sound, they get wet. If they haven't prepared their bedroll, they get cold. If they haven't planned their food, they get hungry. If competently run by staff who genuinely care about the teenagers, these experiences are invaluable. However, because some wilderness experiences are run by callous and unscrupulous operators, check this option out carefully.

Asked about how they teach resident students about the hazards of drug use, one counselor explained,

> We help them see that they can have a good time without doing drugs and that getting high on drugs is only a compensation for not getting high on life. There have to be highs. So we create them by doing wholesome things that are fun. We take them on all sorts of activities and teach them how to enjoy life, how to have fun. We take them on camp-outs so they can learn how to enjoy nature and how to interact with peers in a better atmosphere than they're used to.

These are natural highs that don't have toxic side effects like drugs do. They're genuine.

Clear goals. Outcome behaviors should be clearly specified and used to guide program activities. One program specifies these behavioral goals:

- a feeling of self-worth ("I'm all right, I'm worthwhile; my looks, mental abilities, etc. are okay")
- skills in dealing with others (knowing how to talk and negotiate without manipulating others or struggling for power)
- good school performance (improved attendance, better grades, a positive influence on others, care of books and materials, ability to study and to stick with an assignment until completion)
- good personal management skills (keeping oneself and one's area clean and attractive); dress and grooming habits acceptable to staff and peers
- respect for property (taking care of personal and school property such as clothing, bedding, books, etc.)
- control of temper (dealing with frustrations or anger in ways acceptable to self and others; not jeopardizing one's future standing with others)
- self-control of appetites (exercising and eating well, abstaining from alcohol, tobacco, and other drugs)
- a positive work ethic (being able to do physical labor and feel good about it; understanding that physical work is good for the body and the mind)
- commitment to the values of honesty, loyalty, cleanliness, and trustworthiness (being morally responsible and having acceptable relationships with others of the same and opposite sex)
- worthwhile career goals (developing plans for a successful occupation) (Sorenson's Ranch School, 1999)

Meet with program staff and speak with parents of youngsters who are currently in, or were formerly in, that program to learn whether the staff personally conform to these ideals. Don't enroll your youngster unless you feel that staff members are people you want your youngster to emulate.

Asked how a parent can select a good residential program, a director replied,

> Find a program that fits the needs of your child. Usually they need love and somebody who cares. Make a site visit and get a feeling for the program and its staff. Look for a program whose staff genuinely care about people and will help you evaluate the needs of your child. We're pretty rustic out here, but parents like the feeling of this program, and ninety-nine percent of those who come here to visit send their adolescent.

The personal values reinforced in a treatment program should be specified. These illustrate the aims of one program:

- Recognize that the only people who will always be there for you are your parents.
- Like yourself as a necessary prerequisite to being able to love others and be loved by them.
- Have loyalty to and respect for others, as is shown by listening to them.
- Recognize that the experiences of others can help you avoid repeating their mistakes.
- Be aware that use of alcohol and other drugs is self-defeating behavior.
- Recognize that sexual promiscuity is also self-defeating behavior that may lead to emotional turmoil and health problems.
- Know that the more you help others, the more others will help you; you must be a friend to have a friend; if you are dishonest with others, they are more likely to be dishonest with you; and if you take things that are not yours, you surround yourself with a world of thieves.
- Do for others what you would want them to do for you—only do it first.
- Learn to understand others. It's hard to dislike somebody you know and understand; if you can put yourself in their position, and see things from their point of view, you will comprehend their actions and probably grow to like them (Sorenson's Ranch School, 1999).

Reasonable cost. The program should fit your budget. What does the program cost? How much of the bill will your insurance cover? What happens when the insurance money runs out? Are there relatives who can help out? Beware of programs that charge exorbitant amounts. If the program is too expensive, your youngster won't be there long enough for it to do much good. Some desperate parents go deeply into debt to sign on with ineffective programs because they aren't aware of other options. One couple mortgaged their home to pay for a three-week program for their daughter. To the parents' chagrin, the staff were unwilling to consult with them or provide information. "We can't release confidential information," they were told.

Community reentry plan. The program needs an effective community reentry program with clearly defined steps. During the first few weeks of the program, youngsters may be denied access to their parents, whom they easily manipulate. They must earn the privilege of contacting their parents (phone calls, etc.). Later, parents can visit the facility, and eventually youngsters can visit home. During the interim, program staff help parents create a home environment consistent with effective parental management (that is, clear expectations and consequences for good and bad behavior).

Peer support. The program should have a peer-leadership and peer-counseling component. Older participants who have "learned the ropes" can help newer kids succeed. They can also provide "righteous peer pressure" to counteract the unwholesome influences of drug-using friends. Drug rehabilitation won't work unless your teen completely severs ties with old drug-using associates. Some programs encourage kids to cut off ties with these former friends with formal letters indicating that they aren't using drugs anymore and therefore won't be associating with those individuals.

Appropriate discipline. The program should have an effective discipline program that does *not* include physical and emotional abuse. Beware of programs that use harsh techniques to subdue youngsters. There should be no unusual punishment, infliction of pain, humiliation, intimidation, ridicule, coercion, threats, or mental abuse. Nor should there be anything that interferes with daily living functions such as eating, sleeping, or bathroom use.

Successful programs discipline kids by taking away privileges or using "time-out" procedures, not inflicting cruel punishment. One program requires rebellious kids to sit outside (weather permitting) about fifty feet away from the treatment center to do some thinking. "We cannot force or use physical punishment, but we can wait out a student's mood," said a staff member. "Usually a compromise can be reached and a student chooses an alternative that he's had a part in devising that will aid his development."

"The most important feature of a successful program," said a residential program counselor,

> is to be consistent in what we do. Disciplining must be fair to everyone. It works best if students choose their own discipline, and they usually choose one that is harder than an adult would have chosen. If a kid is stealing, we call him in, remind him that he has broken a bottom-line rule, and ask, "What do you think would be fair?" He may say, "I shouldn't go to activities for a month," or "give me ten hours of service," or "not receive my allowance." The whole key to disciplining is to be fair.

When asked, "What do you do if he won't cooperate, won't say anything?" this counselor replied,

> Well, we give him time to think about it. I may say, "Here are some options. Think about it and come back tomorrow and we'll talk. Think about what we ought to do to help you change your behavior." Unless he is part of the change, it's just another rule. But if he's part of the plan, he feels it's fair and is more inclined to grow from the experience.

Fair discipline involves two concepts: (1) the rules apply to everyone, and (2) the discipline must be tailored to the individual. That's why it's so important to let each student help determine what is fair. For instance, a staff member at a rural center explained,

> It wouldn't be fair for a person who weighs ninety pounds to work all day hauling hay, but it is for someone who weighs a hundred and fifty pounds and has muscle. Each kid has an inward fairness meter and each must be treated individually. We involve each one in the process of whatever we are doing.

Enrolling

How do you tell your teen you've enrolled him in a treatment program? They are rarely eager to enter. Don't act too quickly. Your plan should be carefully thought out, not a spur-of-the-moment decision made during a crisis.

The recovery process that is about to begin is always painful. But when kids and parents face reality together, recovery is possible. "Parents don't have all the answers," a program director noted, "and you never need to feel guilty." When one mother—president of a teacher's association and lecturer on parent-child relations—enrolled her daughter in a drug-treatment program, she told the director, "You don't know how hard it is for me, with the kind of work I do, to bring my daughter here." "It's all right," he responded. "We parents do the best we can. Sometimes we need a little help."

A C T I V I T I E S   F O R   P A R E N T S   A N D   K I D S

21.1 Discuss what you've learned as a family by reading this book and participating in the activities.

21.2 Each family member lists three fun family activities (e.g., shooting baskets in the driveway) and three fun personal activities (e.g., having a friend stay overnight). Then list three serious family activities (e.g., writing a group letter to grandparents) and three serious personal activities (e.g., sorting books, toys, and clothes that will go to charity). Share the family ideas and selected individual ideas. What are family members' favorites? How and when can you implement them?

21.3 Buy one of those giant boxes of sixty-four crayons and get some big pieces of paper. Read this poem from Langston Hughes together, and then have each person draw a picture of one or more dreams. Display everyone's pictures on the refrigerator or family-room wall for a week! Discuss your dreams with each other.

Dreams

Hold fast to dreams
For if dreams die
Life is a broken-winged bird
That cannot fly.
Hold fast to dreams
For when dreams go
Life is a barren field
Frozen with snow

(Hughes, 1994)

From THE COLLECTED POEMS OF LANGSTON HUGHES by Langston Hughes, © 1994 by The Estate of Lanston Hughes. Used by permission of Alfred A. Knopf, a division of Random House. Inc.

REFERENCES

Hughes, Langston. 1994. *The Dream Keeper and Other Poems.* New York: Alfred A. Knopf.
Mecca, Andrew. 1994. "Evaluating Recovery Services: The California Drug and Alcohol Treatment Assessment, Executive Summary Fact Sheet." Press release, State of California Department of Alcohol and Drug Programs, Sacramento, August 29.
Sorenson Ranch School. 1999. Koosharem, Utah.

INTERNET SOURCES

www.tasc.com/charitiy/khk

REMEMBER THIS

There are so many societal forces making alcohol and other drugs enticing that you can't take a passive role and just hope for the best. Plan and practice firm, loving parenting. Teach your children how to handle themselves with good sense. And, get involved in school and community prevention efforts. No, this won't make you a perfect parent, but your efforts *can* make a difference.

The following summarizes the key points discussed in this book.

- Most teenagers experiment with alcohol, tobacco, and marijuana because these substances are easily available and widely glamorized.
- Several giant industries encourage drug use.
- Youngsters escalate into increased levels of drug use when using becomes more rewarding than abstaining.
- Psychoactive drugs promote two kinds of highs: (1) a chemically induced euphoria, and (2) social acceptance by drug-using friends. Some people also use drugs to cope with painful feelings.
- Your challenge as a parent is to help your kids gain highs in healthy ways. Youth who regularly experience natural highs rarely, if ever, escalate into full-blown chemical dependency.
- The ultimate natural high for youths is to feel valued by their parents, siblings, friends, and other significant people in their lives.
- You can help your children achieve natural highs by clearly defining desired behaviors and then consistently rewarding them when they comply.
- Help your children succeed in approved youth activities. Successful experiences with their peers promote healthy adsolescent development.
- Develop a family constitution that spells out your goals, including an agreed-on position on alcohol and other drug use.
- Your actual *behavior* regarding tobacco, alcohol, and other mood-altering drugs exerts a far stronger impact on your kids than anything you say.
- Home should be a safe and rewarding place where kids feel cared for and protected. A healthy family shares traditions and activities together and avoids criticism. One harsh home-scene can outweigh many positive ones.
- Your influence is strongest when your children want to emulate you. Interpersonal bonds grow stronger during your kids' childhood when you spend time together, and when you are sympathetic, understanding, and kind (smiling, touching, praising, listening).

- You can heighten your influence on your kids by participating in school, religious, and community activities that encourage positive youthful choices, such as associating with drug-abstaining friends.
- Don't wait until problems occur to enroll in a parent-training workshop. Parenting challenges even the most effective mothers and fathers.
- When kids begin to spiral into deeper levels of drug involvement, reach out to parent-support groups, family therapy, twelve-step programs, and perhaps a drug-treatment program.
- When a residential treatment program is necessary, select one that has a strong family-oriented approach, one that will involve you and prepare your youth for the return home.
- Most important, remember that even the best parents have problems and that *no parent who keeps trying is a failure!*

How Are Alcohol and Other Drugs Affecting Your Life?

A Self-Test for Teenagers

[See Chapter 3]

YES	NO	1. Do you use alcohol or other drugs to build self-confidence?
YES	NO	2. Do you ever drink or get high immediately after you have a problem at home or at school?
YES	NO	3. Have you ever missed school because of alcohol or other drugs?
YES	NO	4. Does it bother you if someone says that you use too much alcohol or other drugs?
YES	NO	5. Have you started hanging out with a heavy-drinking or drug-using crowd?
YES	NO	6. Are alcohol or other drugs affecting your reputation?
YES	NO	7. Do you feel guilty or depressed after using alcohol or other drugs?
YES	NO	8. Do you feel more at ease on a date when drinking or using other drugs?
YES	NO	9. Have you gotten into trouble at home for using alcohol or other drugs?
YES	NO	10. Do you borrow money or "do without" other things to buy alcohol and other drugs?
YES	NO	11. Do you feel a sense of power when you use alcohol or other drugs?
YES	NO	12. Have you lost friends since you started using alcohol or other drugs?

YES　　NO　　**13.** Do your friends use less alcohol or other drugs than you do?

YES　　NO　　**14.** Do you drink or use other drugs until your supply is all gone?

YES　　NO　　**15.** Do you ever wake up and wonder what happened the night before?

YES　　NO　　**16.** Have you ever been arrested or hospitalized because of alcohol or use of illicit drugs?

YES　　NO　　**17.** Do you ignore any studies or lectures about alcohol or illicit drug use?

YES　　NO　　**18.** Do you think you have a problem with alcohol or other drugs?

YES　　NO　　**19.** Has there ever been someone in your family with a drinking or other drug problem?

YES　　NO　　**20.** Could you have a problem with alcohol or other drugs?

Purchase or public possession of alcohol is illegal for anyone under the age of 21 anywhere in the United States. Aside from the fact that you may be breaking the law by using alcohol and/or illicit drugs, if you answer "yes" to any three of the above questions, you may be at risk for developing alcoholism and/or dependence on another drug. If you answer "yes" to five of these questions, you should seek professional help immediately.

Source: www.ncadd.org/facts/youth1.html

Fallacies or Deceptive "Logic"

[See Activity 2 in Chapter 8]

1. *Appeal to the People.* This advertising principle relies on peer pressure, with very little regard for the product's actual quality or its place in your life. Examples:

- *Bandwagon:*
  "Everybody else is wearing our jeans—you should, too, so you'll be socially acceptable." [Ask, "Who is 'everybody' besides the company's paid models, and do I like your product or need it to prove I'm okay?"]
- *Vanity:*
  "This beautiful model uses our make-up; if you use it, you can be beautiful like her." [Remind yourself, "A little make-up might be nice, but it will not make me look like anyone but myself with make-up on. What do I think of this product, really?"]
- *Snobbery:*
  "Only a select few get to drive this elegant car." [Would the "select few" consist simply of *anyone* who has enough money to buy the car?]

2. *Poisoning the Well,* or Argument against the Person. This technique, a favorite of politicians (it's known as mud-slinging in the political arena), asks you to reject the product's competitors. To avoid lawsuits, most advertisers do this in vague or general ways. Examples:

- "My opponent is a liar, so you can't believe anything he says." [Ask, "How do I know *you're* not lying?"]
- "Watch how poorly this other product cleans your dirty shirt compared to ours." [What "other product" are they using, and how? Is this a fair, scientific experiment?]

3. *Appeal to Unqualified Authority,* as in using celebrities to sell products. (Remember: Just because you like a particular celebrity does not mean that his or her opinion about a product should carry any weight.) Examples:

"Your favorite movie star drinks our juice, so you should too." [Ask, "What if I don't like how your juice tastes? My favorite movie star is a

183

good actor, but his opinions on juice are simply opinions—and paid for, at that!"]

4. *Hasty Generalization.* With this tactic, advertisers use only a few examples to "prove" a sweeping generalization. Examples:

   ■ "Mrs. Jones and Mrs. Smith switched to our painkiller, and their headaches cleared up much faster than with their old painkillers." [Even if the two of them aren't actors and what they say is true, do their two experiences actually prove anything?]

5. *False Cause,* or falsely connecting one event to another. (Remember: Just because one event occurs before another does not mean the first *caused* the second.) Example:

   ■ "I started using this shampoo, and then I won my first beauty pageant!" [Maybe the woman had been training for pageants for years. Also, the shampoo company probably paid her to say this.]

6. *False Dichotomy.* The advertiser presents two ideas as if they were mutually exclusive, but they aren't, necessarily. Example:

   ■ "Either brush with our toothpaste or your teeth will turn yellow." [This is sometimes presented in the form of a threat: "If you don't x then y." But aren't there other products that can also keep your teeth clean?]

7. *Suppressed Evidence.* The advertiser withholds important information that might change your opinion. Example:

   ■ "This beautiful used car has a powerful engine and is in fine working condition!" [It might run today—but a couple of key components will probably wear out in the next month or so.]

8. *Begging the Question or Circular Argument.* The advertiser repeats its message in different words in order to avoid having to make a real case for a product or opinion. Example:

   ■ "This toy is the greatest because it's the best!" [Same difference!]

9. *Vague, Misleading, or Incomplete Language.* Examples:
   ■ "Our vacuum is better!" [Better than what?]
   ■ "More whitener!" [More than what?]
   ■ "It's life-altering!" [In what way? The incomplete phrasing might sound good, but doesn't really tell you much of anything.]

A Quick Test

Now that you've "got the goods" on advertisers, can you spot the fallacies in the following arguments attempting to persuade you to use drugs, cigarettes, or alcohol?

- **a.** "I like it, and you're my friend, so you'll like it, too."
- **b.** "This stuff will blast your brains!"
- **c.** "If you don't, you're no fun."
- **d.** "Everyone does it."
- **e.** "Sarah started drinking, and now she's really popular."
- **f.** "Your parents don't want you to have fun. Don't listen to them."
- **g.** "Jamie is only inviting a few people, and you're one of them."

Answers

- **a.** Unqualified Authority [Respond with, "We may have a lot in common, but I still have my own interests and choices."]
- **b.** Vague or Misleading Language [Ask yourself, "Do I really want my brains 'blasted,' whatever that means?"]
- **c.** False Dichotomy [Ask the person, "You mean, you personally think I would be more fun company for you if I did what *you* wanted, not what I want?"]
- **d.** Bandwagon [Ask, "Who's everyone? Everyone at this party? Everyone except the designated drivers? Everyone whose opinion you think I should care about?"]
- **e.** False Cause [Answer, "Yes, and Sarah also made the cheerleading squad and her aunt bought her a new wardrobe. Also, who exactly are 'the popular people,' and would I really want to hang out with them?"]
- **f.** Poisoning the Well [Ask yourself, "Okay, so it seems as if this accusation about my parents is true sometimes, but do they *really* not want me to ever have fun? Or do they want me to avoid things like alcoholism, lung cancer, and teen pregnancy?"]
- **g.** Snobbery [Respond with, "So? Maybe I don't *like* Jamie or the other people he's inviting, or maybe I don't like how they spend their time."]

Finally, some provocative questions about jeans and soft-drink ads—you know, the ones that say, "Be original. Be different. Use our product." Is this "Snob Appeal," "Bandwagon," or both? How do advertisers take advantage of the tradition of adolescents' rebelling against their parents and society? Why is rebellion a tradition? How can your teens use rebellion to their advantage rather than having it used against them by advertisers, peers, and other influences who have their own agendas and who *don't* have your teens' best interests at heart?

Adapted from Hurley, Patrick J. 1994. *A Concise Introduction to Logic,* 5th edition. Belmont, CA: Wadsworth Publishing, pp. 116–157.

APPENDIX C

Making a Family Message and Calendar Center

[See Activity 4 in Chapter 9]

Gather a large bulletin board; thumb tacks or push pins; small, spiral-bound notepad; string; pencil or pen; and a calendar with large squares for writing schedules.

Remove the front cover from the notepad. Attach the back cover firmly to the bulletin board. Wrap or tape string around one end of the pen or pencil. Attach the other end permanently to the bulletin board. (Family members can now easily use the paper and pencil to jot down phone messages, tear them off the pad, and immediately attach them to the bulletin board.) Discuss message-taking procedures and emphasize their importance. Have each family member write their scheduled activities on the calendar. At the first of each month, schedule family activities and write them in calendar. Coordinate weekly.

Source: Family Connections Home Learning Guide, n.d. Utah State University Extension, Logan, UT 84322.

Safety Tips for Internet Use

[See Chapter 10]

Here are a few safety tips, provided by the FBI Educational Web Publications, to keep your child's on-line experience safe. Instruct your kids to practice the following guidelines:

- Never give out identifying information such as name, home address, school name, or telephone number in a public-message forum such as a chat room or an on-line bulletin board. Never send a person a picture of yourself without first checking with your parent or guardian.

- Never respond to messages or bulletin board items that are:
  suggestive,
  obscene,
  belligerent,
  threatening, or that
  make you feel uncomfortable.

- Be careful when someone offers you something for nothing, such as gifts and money. Be *very* careful about any offers that involve your going to a meeting or having someone visit your home.

- Tell your parent or guardian right away if you come across any information that makes you feel uncomfortable.

- Never arrange a face-to-face meeting with someone without telling your parent or guardian. If your parent or guardian agrees to the meeting, make sure that you meet in a public place, and have a parent or guardian with you.

- Remember that people you meet on-line may not be who they seem. Because you can't see or hear them, it would be easy for these individuals to misrepresent themselves. Thus, someone indicating that "she" is a "twelve-year-old girl" could, in reality, be an older man looking to meet young girls.

- Be sure that you are dealing with someone that you and your parents know and trust before giving out any personal information about yourself through e-mail.

- Get to know your "on-line friends" just as you get to know all of your other friends.

Should you become aware that your child has stumbled across any pornographic or indecent materials involving children or adolescents, or has experienced any other potentially dangerous incidents on-line, immediately notify your local FBI office or contact the National Center for Missing and Exploited Children at www.missingkids.com/cybertip or 1-800-843-5678.

Source: www.smartparent.com/safety.htm

APPENDIX E

Blocking and Software

[See Chapter 10]

Several software programs exist that can help you control the Internet content available to your children. Most of these programs, listed below with Web sites where you can learn about them, perform one or more of the following functions: (1) block access to adult sites, (2) rate sites based on "adult content" (pornography, violence/profanity, intolerance, militant extremism, gambling, drug culture, etc.), (3) establish time controls for individual users (for example, blocking usage after a particular time at night, or during established homework times), and (4) log surfing activities (allowing parents to see which sites a child has visited).

- Bess: www.n2h2.com/
- BrownseSafe: www.browsesafe.com
- CleanWeb: www.cleanweb.net/
- Click & Browse, Jr.: www.netwavelink.com/html/junior.html
- Crayon Crawler: www.crayoncrawler.com/
- Cyber Patrol: www.cyberpatrol.com
- CyberSitter: www.cybersitter.com/
- CyberSnoop: www.pearlsw.com/csnoop3/snoop.htm
- Disk Tracy: www.disktracy.com/
- ENUFF: www.akrontech.com/
- Exotrope: www.exotrope.com/
- Family Connect: www.familyconnect.com/
- GreenBox: www.greenbox.net
- Guardianet: www.guardianet.net/home.htm
- GuardOne: www.guardone.com
- I-Gear: www.urlabs.com/
- Integrity Online: www.integrityonline2.com/kids.htm
- InterGate Web Filtering Service: www.Internetproducts.com/products/filtering/
- InterQuick's SmartFilter: www.smartfilter.interquick.com/
- The Internet Filter: www.turnercom.com/if/
- KidSafe Explorer: www.arlington.com.au/
- KNC Software: www.kncsoftware.com
- NetNanny: www.netnanny.com
- NetRated: www.netrated.com

- Orbit Net: www.orbitnet.net/
- Safe-Net Mail: www.maiasoftware.com/safenet/
- Save Our System: www.sos.sterlingweb.com
- Specs for Kids: www.view.planetweb.com/cust/ss_lvll.html
- SurfMonkey: www.surfmonkey.com/
- Surf on the Safe Side: www.surfonthesafeside.com/
- Surf Watch: www.surfwatch.com/
- Triple Exposure: www.ips-corp.com/tripleex.htm
- Two Dog Net: www.twodognet.com/
- Virtual Gate: www.virtual-gate.com
- WebChaperone with iCRT: www.webchaperone.com/
- We-Blocker: www.we-blocker,com/
- Web Sense: www.websense.com
- WinGuardian: www.webroot.com/chap1.htm
- WinWhatWhere For Families: www.winwhatwhere.com
- WizGuard: www.wizguard.com
- X-Stop: www.xstop.com/
- X-Detect: www.xdetect.com/
- ZeekSafe: www.zeeks.com/ZeekSafe/ZeekSafeMain.asp

On-line Service and Internet Service Providers

Another option for parents who want to control what their kids see on-line is to sign up with an Internet service provider (ISP) that restricts access to sites inappropriate for children. Some ISPs are geared toward family access and provide mechanisms parents can use to restrict their children's Internet use. Such providers include the following:

- AOL: www.aol.com. If you are an AOL member and would like to set restrictions on your kids' Internet browsing, go to keyword "parental," choose the screen name you want to restrict, click on teen or child access, and follow the on-line instructions.
- BriteSite: www.britesite.net/services/index.asp
- CleanWeb: www.cleanweb.net/
- ClearSail.Net: www.clearsail.net/
- Crystal Internet: www.gotocrystal.net/filtering/info.html
- Dotsafe, Inc.: www.dotsafe.net
- eschoolhouse: www.eschoolhouse.com/
- Family Safe Internet: www.family-safe.net/
- Family's Choice Internet: www.familyschoice.com
- InnoSence Net: www.innosence.net

- Integrity Online: www.integrityonline2.com/kids.htm
- Mayberry USA: www.mayberryusa.net
- MSN: www.msn.com
- Mindspring: www.earthlink.com/content/family/
- Porn Blocker: www.PornBlocker.com
- Prodigy: www.prodigy.com. Prodigy recommends that its members download CyberPatrol software and use this in conjunction with their children's use of the Prodigy service.
- Rated-G Online: www.rated-g.com. Server-based solutions that restrict, block, and "filter" pornography and other content deemed inappropriate.
- SafeAccess.Net: www.safeaccess.net/
- TrustedNet: www.trusted.net/
- QualityNet: www.qualitynet.org/about.html
- U.S. LocalNet: www.uslocalnet.com

Additional Resources

In addition to blocking and filtering software, there are other ways to monitor your children's on-line activities. The sites listed below can help you gather more information about some of these products.

- ComputerCop: www.computercopinfo.com/
- SaveMail: www.savemail.com
- Sentry Cam: www.sentrycam.com
- MoM: www.avsweb.com/mom/index.html
- Line Loc: www.members.tripod.com/
- Chat Minder: www.chatminder.com/
- Chat Nanny: www.chatnanny.com
- SoftEyes: www.softeyes.com
- Spector Software: www.spectorsoft.com/

Source: www.smartparent.com/protect.htm

Family Councils

[See Activity 4 in Chapter 10]

Here are some family-council guidelines:

- *Set a regular time.* Having a regular time and place for family-council meetings gives the council a position of importance and makes it a permanent part of family operations. If teens know that the family meets together regularly, they can feel confident that most of their problems can wait a few days to be discussed. For this reason, some families like weekly meetings.
- *Use an agenda.* During the week, post a piece of paper on which family members can list concerns they want brought up at council. During the next meeting, discuss things in the order listed on the paper. This process also reduces the number of problems that crop up between meetings. Parents can say, "List it on the agenda, and we'll discuss it at the next meeting."
- *Make attendance voluntary.* Although all members of the family are invited to attend, attendance should not be forced. However, absent members are still expected to abide by any decisions made by the family council.
- *Ensure that each person has equal voice.* Everyone should be encouraged to contribute ideas and suggestions. Treat all members the same, regardless of age. Introduce the problem, discuss solutions, and then vote on a solution—all while giving everyone a chance to get involved. Remember that councils do not always run smoothly. Teenagers may be suspicious that this new program is just another way for parents to gain teens' compliance to demands. In your first few council meetings, youngsters may test parents to see whether they are sincere about including them in family decision-making.
- *Use rules of order.* If participation is to be equal, you need a way to maintain order. If all family members have the right to express themselves, then they also have the right to be heard—which implies that others have the obligation to listen.
- *Rotate chairmanship.* If the same person conducts all meetings, that person eventually begins to assume an air of superiority. To help maintain a feeling of equality, let family members take turns conducting the

councils. Each person can then experience the privileges and the responsibilities of this position.

- *Accentuate solutions.* Family councils are not just "gripe sessions"— times to get together and complain. To prevent unproductive griping, ensure that the person presenting a problem also suggests at least one possible solution. Family members can then discuss alternative solutions or modify the one presented.

In practice, some solutions do not work as well as anticipated. As family members begin to live with a decision, they may decide it needs to be changed. However, wait until the next regular meeting to make the change. Children can soon recognize a need for better solutions, and they learn through experience to make wiser choices. When family-council meetings are held regularly, each member learns to project ahead and anticipate problems. When this occurs, the emphasis at council meetings shifts from problem solving to problem prevention and planning.

Family council can also be a time to plan fun things such as vacations or family outings. Talk about different places to visit and how to spend the time available.

The family council can serve as the final authority for the family, or a family can use a modified version of decision-making. For the council to be effective, however, most decisions made by the council need to be binding. If parents always overrule the council, children will soon lose interest.

Keep a record. Sometimes a difference of opinion can arise over who conducted the last meeting, what matters the family discussed, and what plans people agreed on. For this reason, recording minutes is most helpful. The secretary can rotate with each meeting.

Adapted from Family Connections Home Learning Guide, n.d. Utah State University Extension, Logan, UT 84322.

APPENDIX G

Oral Histories

[See Activity 4 in Chapter 12]

Grandparents, great-grandparents, and older relatives love to talk about their memories. By listening to them, we understand what their lives were like and learn about our own heritage. Make a tape recording of older family members' stories to capture the past and create a cherished family possession.

Here's What to Do

- Arrange in advance to interview someone in your family.
- Set up a time and a quiet place for the interview. (*Note:* Be sure to choose a place where you won't be disturbed by other people, or by background noise that would spoil the quality of the tape recording.)
- Make a list of questions you want to ask. Choose questions that prompt a story, not those that can be answered with a simple yes or no. (See sample questions below.)

Sample Questions

About You

What were you like when you were my age? What did you do for fun? Did you ever get into mischief? If so, what kind? What kinds of toys did you play with as a child? Did you have a pet? If so, what was it? What were your parents like? Did you ever get mad at them? If so, when? What was it like going to school? Where were you born? Where did you grow up? What do you remember about the house you grew up in? Did your family ever move? If so, where, and why? Did you have brothers and sisters? If so, how did you get along with them? Do you think life was easier when you were my age? If so, in what sense? When did you meet Grandma/Grandpa? What was your first date with her/him like? What was she/he like back then? Tell me about Mom/Dad when he/she was little. What did your own parents do for a living? What were your own grandparents like? What did they do? How did you celebrate holidays? What foods did you eat? Did your family have any ethnic traditions (customs practiced by people in the country your ancestors came from)? If so, what were they?

About the Times

What do you remember about the Great Depression? Grandpa—were you in World War II? If so, what can you tell me about it? Grandma—what was it like to live through the war? What were you doing when you heard about Pearl Harbor? Did anyone close to you get killed in the war? If so, what can you tell me about him? What did you think of President Roosevelt? Of all the presidents you've known, whom do you think was the best? Why? Did you vote for John F. Kennedy? What were you doing when you found out President Kennedy had been shot? What radio programs did you listen to? When did you buy your first television set? What did you think about the first astronauts' landing on the moon?

About Me

When was the first time you ever saw me? What was I like when I was a baby? Am I like my mom/dad when she/he was young? If so, in what ways? What do you think life will be like when I get to be your age? What predictions do you have of things you think or hope will happen during my lifetime?

Source: Family Connections Home Learning Guide, n.d. Utah State University Extension, Logan, UT 84322.

APPENDIX H

Pick a Card, Any Card

[See Activity 5 in Chapter 12]

Write the following questions and others you choose on three-inch by five-inch cards, place the cards in a stack, and let each family member pick a card and answer the question. Then everyone else responds to the same question. You can use the questions during dinner, on trips in the car, at bedtime, or during visits to grandparents and other relatives.

Agree to these rules: (1) Family members may not make fun of, criticize, or "put down" one another. (2) If people don't want to answer a question, they may choose another one or pass. (3) No one gets pressured into participating in this activity.

- Who are you?
- What movie title best describes your life?
- If someone were to write a book about you, what do you think he or she would call it?
- If someone could give you anything in the world for your birthday, what would you like it to be?
- If you could invite a famous person to dinner, who would it be? Why?
- What is the strangest thing you ever ate?
- If you could go back in time, when would you have wanted to live?
- If you could change your age, what age would you rather be?
- If you were convinced that reincarnation was a fact, how would you like to come back?
- Name two famous people you'd like to have over.
- If you were a doctor, what ailment would you most like to cure?
- What book would you recommend to everyone?
- Make a statement about success.
- What three things about your life would you like to change?
- How do you feel about growing old?
- If you were going to be any vegetable, which one would you be and why?
- What European city would you most prefer to live in?
- How would you define joy?
- In one line, what is life all about?
- What's your favorite snack to eat at a movie?
- What's your earliest childhood memory?

- If you received a large research grant, what question would you research?
- What's your favorite food for breakfast?
- What's the best birthday present you ever received? Gave?
- What's your favorite music?
- If you could be appointed ambassador to any country, which country would you choose? Why?
- If you could date any movie star, who would it be?
- What's your favorite book, ever?
- What's your most memorable birthday?
- What things make your life complicated?
- If you could be an animal/bird, which one would you be?
- What talents do you have? (Don't be modest!)
- What kind of food do you most like to eat late at night?
- What would you like to be remembered for after you die?
- Give one word to describe the person next to you.
- If you wrote a book today, what would the title be?
- What is your favorite song?
- Say something about earthquakes.
- If you could take only three people with you on a trip around the world, whom would you take? Why?
- If you could live any place in the world, where would it be?
- How would you describe peace?
- If you received five thousand dollars as a gift, how would you spend it?
- What planet would you most like to visit? Why?
- What is the most boring thing you can imagine doing?
- What is the most interesting thing about you?
- If you could choose another name for yourself, what would it be?
- If you were president of a planet, what would be the first rule you would make?
- If your bedroom were on fire and you had time to grab only one thing, what would it be?
- If you could be invisible for a day, what would you do?
- What talent do you most wish you had?
- What TV or movie star would you like to invite to your birthday party?
- What would you do if you had a "magic wand"?
- What's your favorite thing to do on Saturday night?
- Who are you?
- What's your favorite dessert?
- What's your favorite flower?
- What do you do in your spare time?

- If you could be a character from any book or short story, who would it be?
- What kind of movies do you like best?
- If you could change your age, what age would you rather be?
- What food did you hate most when you were a little kid? Did you ever try to secretly get rid of it without your parents knowing?
- What kind of trophy would you like to win?
- What is something that really "bugs" you?

Source: Family Connections Home Learning Guide, n.d. Utah State University Extension, Logan, UT 84322.

Refusal Skills

[See Activity 4 in Chapter 13]

Practice learning to say *no*.

Learning good refusal skills can help you in all sorts of difficult social situations you may face during your lifetime. Becoming comfortable setting limits for yourself and feeling natural as you say no to outside pressure will help you stay out of undesirable situations, as well as increase your self-confidence and self-esteem.

When practicing refusal skills and discussing personal situations, keep these basic rules in mind:

- Respect others' opinions.
- Avoid putting others down.
- Respect privacy and don't disclose information about others that could hurt them.
- Let others finish what they're saying before you speak.

Refusal skills include the following:

- Asking questions ("What are we going to do? What are you asking me to do?")
- Naming the trouble ("That's stealing.")
- Stating the consequences ("If I smoked with you I would not feel good about myself, and I could get kicked off the team.")
- Suggesting an alternative ("Instead of that, why don't we. . . ?")
- Encouraging the person to consider changing his or her mind ("Are you sure you want to do that?")
- Staying connected ("If you change your mind, I'll be at the field/home," etc.)

Under pressure, be sure to:

- Stay calm. Remind yourself that "disagreeing with others or saying no does not necessarily mean they'll stop liking me—even if it seems like it at the time. If I say no to other people and they get angry or upset, that doesn't mean that I should have said yes. My rights are important, too."
- Take a deep breath.

When a person keeps pushing you:

- Say the person's name and make eye contact. State your reasons for saying "no."
- Say, "Listen to me."
- Pause to see whether the person is listening.
- Leave, saying, "I'll see you later."

Source: www.kickbutt.org/youth/factguide/42.html

Organizations, Helplines, and Internet Resources

[See Introduction to Part Seven]

Many hospitals, community colleges, and other organizations offer classes for parents that are designed to improve communication and understanding between children and parents. Consult your local library, school, or community-service organization for more information.

Organizations

Alcoholics Anonymous (AA) World Services, 475 Riverside Drive, New York, NY 10115. This worldwide organization, a fellowship of men and women who come together to share their experiences with alcoholism, helps alcoholics achieve sobriety. You can reach AA by phone at 212-870-3400 (for literature) or 212-647-1680 (for meetings.) Or, see your telephone White Pages.

Al-Anon/Alateen Family Group Headquarters, P.O. Box 862, Midtown State, NY, 10018–0862. Established as a resource for family members and friends of alcoholics. Al-Anon is a free, nonprofessional, worldwide organization with more than thirty thousand groups. Call 1-800-356-9996 (for literature) or 1-800-344-2666 (for meetings), or see your telephone White Pages.

American Council for Drug Education. 204 Monroe Street, Rockville, ID 20850. Provides information on drug use, develops media campaigns, reviews scientific findings, publishes books and a newsletter, and offers films and curriculum materials for preteens. Call 301-294-0600.

Chemical People Project. The Public Television Outreach Alliance, c/o WQED-TV, 4802 Fifth Avenue, Pittsburgh, PA 15213. Supplies information in the form of tapes, literature, and seminars. Call 412-391-0900.

Families Anonymous, Inc. Offers a twelve-step, self-help program for families and friends of people with behavioral problems usually associated with drug abuse. A worldwide organization, it is similar to Alcoholics Anonymous. Call 800-736-9805.

Families in Action National Drug Information Center. 2296 Henderson Mill Road, Suite 204, Atlanta, GA 30345. Publishes *Drug Abuse Update,* a quarterly journal of news and information for those interested in drug prevention, $25 for four issues. Call 404-934-6364.

Hazelden Foundation. Pleasant Valley Road, Box 176, Center City, MN 55012–0176. Distributes educational materials and self-help literature for participants in twelve-step recovery programs and for addicted professionals. Call 800-328-9000.

Institute on Black Chemical Abuse. 2614 Nicollet Avenue, Minneapolis, Mn 55408. Provides training and technical assistance to programs that serve African-American clients and others of color. Call 612-871-7878.

"Just Say No" Clubs. 1777 North California Boulevard, Suite 200, Walnut Creek, CA 94596. Provides support and positive peer reinforcement to youth through workshops, seminars, newsletters, and a variety of activities. Call 800-258-2766 or 415-939-6666.

Mothers Against Drunk Driving (MADD). 511 E. John Carpenter Freeway Suite 700, Irving, TX 75062. Their mission is to stop drunk driving, the victims of this violent crime, and prevent underage drinking. A non-profit grass roots organization with more than 600 chapters nationwide, MADD looks for effective solutions to drunk driving and underage drinking problems, while supporting those who have already experienced the pain of these crimes. Call 214-744-6233. For the Victim Hotline, call 800-438-6233.

Nar-Anon Family Group Headquarters. World Service Office, P.O. Box 2562, Palos Verdes Peninsula, CA 90274. Operates in a manner similar to Al-Anon and supports people who have friends or family members with drug problems. Call 310-547-5800.

Narcotics Anonymous (NA). World Service Office, P.O. Box 9999, Van Nuys, CA 91409. A fellowship of men and women, similar to Alcoholics Anonymous, who meet to help one another with their drug-dependency problems. Call 818-773-9999.

National Association for Children of Alcoholics (NACoA). A national nonprofit membership organization working on behalf of children of alcohol and drug dependent parents. Their mission is to advocate for all children and families affected by alcoholism and other drug dependencies. Call 888-554-COAS or access www.nacoa.net.

National Clearinghouse for Alcohol and Drug Information (NCADI). Box 2345, Rockville, MD 20852. Distributes a wide variety of publications dealing with alcohol and other drug abuse. Call 301-468-2600 or 1-800-729-6686.

National Council on Alcoholism, Inc. 12 West 21st Street, New York, NY 10010. A national, voluntary health agency, it provides information about alcoholism and alcohol problems through more than three hundred local affiliates. Call 800-NCA-CALL.

National Crime Prevention Council. 1700 K Street, N.W., Washington, D.C. 20006. Works to prevent crime and drug use by developing materials (audio visual, reproducible brochures, and other publications) for parents and children. Call 202-466-NCPC.

National Families in Action. 2296 Henderson Mill Road, Suite 204, Atlanta, GA 30345. A drug education, prevention, and policy center that focuses on preventing drug use, abuse, addiction, and death and serves as a link between science, law, and the public. Its mission is to help families and communities prevent drug use among children by promoting policies based on science. It maintains a drug-information center for use by the public, maintains an Internet Web site, and publishes numerous articles, pamphlets, books, and a quarterly digest, *Drug Abuse Update.* Call 770-934-6364.

National Federation of Parents for Drug-Free Youth, Inc. Communications Center, 1423 North Jefferson, Springfield, MO 65802. Sponsors the National Red Ribbon Campaign to reduce drug demand. The Responsible Educated Adolescents Can Help (REACH) program educates junior and senior high school students about drug abuse. Call 417-836-3709.

National PTA Drug and Alcohol Abuse Prevention Project. 700 North Rush Street, Chicago, IL 60611. Offers kits, brochures, posters, and other publications on alcohol and other drugs for parents, teachers, and PTA organizations. Call 312-577-4500.

Safe Homes. P.O. Box 702, Livingston, NJ 07039. Encourages parents to sign an agreement stipulating that when parties are held in their home they will adhere to a strict no-alcohol/no-drug-use rule.

Teen-Anon Recovery. P.O. Box 191396, San Francisco, CA 94119. A national twelve-step recovery fellowship for teens dealing with substance abuse of all kinds. Call 415-437-2487 or 877-823-TEEN outside of California.

Toughlove. P.O. Box 1069, Doylestown, PA 18901. A national self-help group for parents, children, and communities that emphasizes cooperation, personal initiative, and action. Toughlove holds workshops and publishes a newsletter, brochures, and books. Call 800-333-1069 or 215-348-7090.

Young & Recovering. The Streetcats Foundation, 267 Lester Avenue, Suite 104, Oakland, CA 94606. A national twelve-step fellowship on college campuses and elsewhere for youth 19–26 recovering from alcohol and other drugs. Call 510-444-6074 or access www.youngandrecovering.8k.com.

Toll-free Numbers

1-800-COCAINE. A Cocaine Helpline. A round-the-clock information and referral service. Recovering cocaine-addict counselors answer the phones, offer guidance, and refer drug users and parents to local public and private treatment centers and family-learning centers.

1-800-342-AIDS. National AIDS Hotline. A service of the Center for Disease Control and Prevention, it is the primary HIV/AIDS information, education, and referral service in the U.S. Professional AIDS information specialists answer questions about HIV transmission and prevention, HIV testing, and HIV/AIDS treatments. Individual questions are answered in a confidential manner and callers receive referrals to national, state, and local HIV/AIDS service organizations. It also provides a number of publications and posters in Spanish and English which are available in print or online.

1-800-662-HELP. Center for Substance Abuse Treatment Referral Service, of the U.S. Department of Health and Human Services. A confidential information and referral line that directs callers to substance abuse treatment centers in the local community. This referral service also distributes free materials on drug abuse in response to inquiries.

1-800-NCA-CALL. National Council on Alcoholism Information Line. The National Council on Alcoholism, Inc., a nonprofit organization that combats alcoholism, other drug addictions, and related problems, provides referral services to families and individuals seeking help with alcoholism or other drug problems.

1-800-241-7946. PRIDE Drug Information Hotline. Parent's Resource Institute for Drug Education (PRIDE) refers concerned parents to parent groups in their state or local area, gives information on how parents can form a group in their community, provides telephone consultation and referrals to emergency health centers, and maintains a series of drug-information tapes that callers can listen to, free of charge, by calling after 5:00 P.M.

Internet Sources

High School Center	www.child.net/hscentral.htm
Teen City Central	www.enn2.com/teencity.htm
Teen Surfer	www.teensurfer.com
Kid City Village	www.city.net/kidcity.htm
Kid Surfer	www.kidsurger.org
For Kids & Teens	www.child.net/forkids.htm
Missing Children Center	www.child.net/missing.htm
Volunteer For Kids	www.child.net/volunteer.htm
City Kids and Teens	www.child.net/citykids.htm
Teen Violence Resources	www.child.net/violence.htm
Youth Drug/Alcohol Resource	www.child.net/drugalc.htm
Familysurfer Net Service	www.child.net/internet.htm
National Childrens Coalition	www.child.net/ncc.htm
Streetcats Foundation	www.child.net/street.htm
Cweb College Central	www.enn2.com/cweb.htm
Cityteen	www.child.net/cityteenhtm
National Clearinghouse for Alcohol and Drug Information	www.health.org
Substance Abuse and Mental Health Services Administration	www.samhsa.gov

INDEX